SOUTHEAST ASIAN

COOKING

Menus and recipes from
Thailand, Singapore, Vietnam,
Brunei, Malaysia, Indonesia
and the Philippines

by Barbara Hansen

FISHER
BOOKS

Publishers:	Bill Fisher
	Helen Fisher
	Howard Fisher
Editors:	Veronica Durie
	Helen Fisher
Art Director:	David Fischer
Cover &	
Illustrations:	David Fischer
Book Production:	Paula Peterson

Published by Fisher Books
P. O. Box 38040
Tucson, Arizona 85740-8040
602-292-9080

Copyright 1992 Fisher Books

Printed in U.S.A.
Printing 10 9 8 7 6 5 4 3 2

**Library of Congress
Cataloging-in-Publication Data**

Hansen, Barbara Joan.
    Southeast Asian cooking : menus and recipes from Thailand, Singapore, Vietnam, Brunei, Malalaysia, Indonesia, and the Philippines /by Barbara Hansen.
        p.   cm.
    Includes index.
    ISBN 1-55561-050-1 : $9.95 ($12.95 Can.)
    1. Cookery, Southeast Asian.   I. Title.
TX724.5.S68H35   1992
641.6959—dc20
                                    92-29049
                                    CIP

Notice: The information in this book is true and complete to the best of our knowlege. It is offered with no guarantes on the part of the author or Fisher Books. Author and publisher disclaim all liability in connection with use of this book.

Acknowledgments

Eating my way through Southeast Asia has been an exciting adventure. I've gone from sidewalk meals in Saigon (Ho Chi Minh City) to the palace kitchens of the Sultan of Brunei, from food stalls in Malaysia to a princely residence in Java, from village homes in Bali to luxury hotels in Bangkok and from Chinese noodle shops in Singapore to Malacañang Palace in Manila.

In Los Angeles, where Asian restaurants and markets abound, I've searched out still more wonderful dishes. The result is this book.

I want to thank all the cooks and cooking teachers, food stall and restaurant proprietors, chefs and hotel personnel who have been so generous in sharing their knowledge.

—**Barbara Hansen**

Table of Contents

Introduction

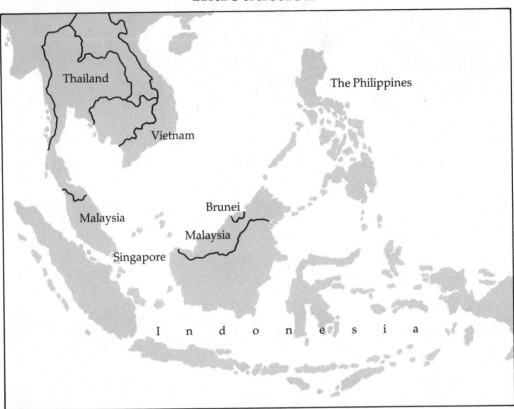

Thailand

The Philippines

Vietnam

Brunei

Malaysia

Malaysia

Singapore

I n d o n e s i a

Southeast Asia

Southeast Asian Cooking will take you on an exciting culinary adventure. The destination may sound exotic, but the journey is easy. Many of the recipes are so simple a novice can handle them with ease. Most of the dishes combine well with Western foods. This means you can add one or two to a familiar menu rather than staging an elaborate—and exhausting—banquet of authentic foods. You'll be rewarded with new tastes that provide a pleasant escape from routine, and fresh ideas for entertaining too.

Southeast Asia's enticing cuisines offer something for everyone. The backyard barbecue chef, the vegetarian, the diet-conscious salad lover, the natural-foods advocate and potluck partygoer will find as much to please them as the kitchen adventurer.

The recipes come from countries that have burst on the international scene with thriving economies and cultural attractions drawing tourists from around the world. Thailand, Singapore, Malaysia, Indonesia, Brunei and the Philippines compose the Association of Southeast Asian Nations (ASEAN). Like these countries, nearby Vietnam offers fine food on every level, from sidewalk stall to serious restaurant.

You'll notice amazing variety. India, China and the Middle East have strongly influenced these cuisines, and the West has left its stamp too. Colonial powers such as Great Britain, France, Spain, Holland, Portugal and the United States modified local dishes to taste and left behind some of their own. This two-way recipe exchange continues today through trade, travel and immigration.

As Southeast Asians resettle around the world, they've opened restaurants and markets, making available ingredients that we haven't seen before. But don't worry if you can't obtain these special seasonings. Often, they can be replaced with common Western ingredients or simply omitted. You'll be relieved to know that quite a few recipes in this book require nothing more exotic than soy sauce.

Try these dishes, and you'll see that Southeast Asian food is light, healthful and as bright as the sun that warms this part of the world so intensely. Best of all, you don't have to travel beyond your own kitchen to enjoy it.

The Ingredients

Southeast Asian cookery requires surprisingly few ingredients beyond those available in a well-equipped supermarket or Asian grocery. Other less common ingredients can be duplicated successfully at home. This list explains the ingredients used in this book and suggests substitutions.

Black fungus
A dried product resembling dried mushrooms, black fungus lacks a pronounced flavor but provides color, contrast and a crunchy texture. Before it is used, it must be soaked until softened, then well drained. Then slice or shred as required.

Candlenuts
These oily nuts are crushed and added to curries and other dishes for flavor and consistency. Asian names are *kemiri* (Indonesia) and *buah keras* (Malaysia). Substitute unsalted macadamia nuts. In some cases almonds may be used.

Chayote
A pale-green, pear-shaped, mild flavored squash. Chayotes are found in Mexican and Latin markets and some supermarkets.

Chinese grass jelly
A dark-brown gelatinous product with little flavor that is used in Southeast Asian drinks and desserts. Canned grass jelly can be purchased in Chinese markets.

Chinese long beans
These slim beans are sometimes called *yard-long beans*. They are similar in taste to fresh green beans with a slightly chewier texture. Substitute fresh green beans.

Chinese sausage
Firm, dry, reddish-colored, fat-marbled sausages with a sweet flavor. They must be cooked before they are eaten.

Cilantro
Fresh coriander, which is also called *Chinese parsley.*

Coconut cream
Coconut cream is the thick first squeezing from freshly grated coconut or the top layer in a can of unshaken coconut milk. Cream of coconut is a commercial sweetened drink mix. The two are not interchangeable.

Coconut milk
This is not the water inside the coconut, but the white liquid squeezed from the shredded coconut.

Curry pastes
The Thais use a variety of curry pastes made of ground chiles and other seasonings. These are available canned in many Asian markets. Recipes for two curry pastes are on pages 15 and 16.

Curry powder

The best curry powder is ground from individual spices and contains no starchy filler. As an alternative, use an imported or a domestic Indian-style curry powder.

Fish sauce

A salty, clear, amber-colored liquid made from fish or shrimp and used as a seasoning and table condiment. Asian names are *nuoc mam* (Vietnam), *nam pla* (Thailand) and *patis* (the Philippines).

Galingal

A knobby root that resembles ginger and is widely used in Southeast Asian cooking. The botanical name is *Alpinia galanga* and the common name in English is *galingal* or *galingale*. In Indonesia it is called *laos*, in Malaysia *lengkuas* and in Thailand *kha*. Used fresh in Southeast Asia, galingal is available elsewhere frozen, dried or powdered and occasionally fresh.

Garam masala

A blend of ground spices used in Indian cooking. Typical components are coriander, cumin, cloves, cinnamon, cardamom and black pepper.

Golden needles

Dried tiger-lily flower buds are named for their shape and dull golden color. They must be soaked in water 30 minutes before using.

Cardamom

Cardamom seeds are encased in pale green shells that have been dried. Most Indian markets carry green cardamom. The pods are added whole to a dish, or the seeds are removed from the shell and then used, depending on the recipe. White cardamom pods are bleached. Either may be used.

Hoisin sauce

A dark-brown, thick, sweet Chinese condiment made from soybeans.

Jícama

A large, brown-skinned, juicy, sweet root vegetable that resembles a turnip in texture. It is stocked in Mexican markets and many supermarkets. Eat it cooked or raw.

Kaffir lime leaves

These are double lime leaves, growing together on a single stem. They have a pronounced flavor and fragrance. Both leaves and peel from the fruit are used. They're sold dried in Asian markets. Regional names for leaves are *bai magrut* or *makrood* (Thailand) and *daun jeruk purut* or *daun limau purut* (Indonesia and Malaysia).

Kangkong

A long-stemmed green that has various names including *water spinach, water convolvulus,* and in Thailand *morning glory vine* or *pak bung*. Spinach can be substituted.

Lemon grass

A long, thick grass with leaves at the top and a solid portion several inches long at the root end. This lower portion is sliced or pounded and used in cooking. Lemon grass has a light, lemonlike flavor and aroma without the tang or bitterness of lemons. It is available fresh, dried and powdered in Southeast Asian markets. Other names are *serai* or *sereh* (Indonesia and Malaysia), *takrai* (Thailand) and *citronella*.

Maggi seasoning

A dark-brown, salty, nutty-flavored liquid used as a condiment in Thai and Vietnamese cooking.

Makhua puong

A Thai name for tiny green eggplants the size of a large pea and refreshingly bitter in flavor. Sometimes they are available fresh in Thai markets. Green peas can be substituted.

Mushrooms

Special types of mushrooms used in Southeast Asian dishes include:

Dried Oriental mushrooms

Dried dark mushrooms that are often called by their Japanese name, *shiitake*. The dried mushrooms must be soaked before using. Fresh shiitake are sometimes available.

Straw mushrooms

Frequently used in Chinese cooking, straw mushrooms have a long cap that resembles a partially opened umbrella. Asian markets stock canned ones. Canned whole button mushrooms may be substituted.

Nata de piña

Also called *pineapple gel* or *pineapple gelatin*, this translucent, delicately flavored substance resembles colorless gelatin and is a nice addition to desserts and fruit salads. The gel is manufactured in the Philippines.

Noodles

Many types of noodles are used in Southeast Asian cookery. Three varieties are used in this book:

Bean-thread noodles

Also called *bean threads, bean vermicelli, cellophane* or *glass noodles*, these dried white noodles resemble rice sticks but are made from mung-bean starch. They soften quickly when soaked.

Fresh rice noodles

Available in areas with large Chinese populations, these come in sheets that have been rolled and cut into strips.

Dried rice noodles

Wiry, thin, white rice noodles are also called *rice sticks* or *rice vermicelli*. These become puffy and crisp when deep-fried or soft when soaked in water. Other rice noodles are flattened and wider.

Oriental eggplant

Long, slim, purple or light-green eggplants. Substitute an equal amount of ordinary eggplant.

Oyster sauce

A thick, brown, salty Chinese seasoning made from oysters and available in Chinese markets.

Palm seeds

Chewy, translucent, white seeds from a variety of palm. Packed in syrup, they're exported from Thailand and the Philippines.

Pandan

A plant with long, spiky green leaves used as a flavoring and a green food coloring. The flavor is reminiscent of butterscotch and is good in desserts. Use dried or fresh leaves. Bottled pandan flavoring comes from Thailand, where the leaves are called *bai toey,* and from Indonesia where it's *daun pandan.*

Rice

When making steamed rice, use long-grain rice rather than converted or instant rice. Special types of rice for Asian cooking include:

Basmati rice

A superior grade of rice produced in India and Pakistan. It's long-grained with a nutty flavor.

Glutinous rice

A short-grain rice that becomes very sticky when cooked. Often used in desserts, it is sometimes called *sticky rice* or *sweet rice.* Glutinous rice is also made into flour. Black glutinous rice is a dark-colored variety.

Rice wine

Wine made from fermented rice. Examples are Japanese *sake* and Chinese rice wine. Do not use *mirin,* which is sweetened rice wine. A dry sherry can sometimes be substituted.

Sambal oelek

A very hot Indonesian seasoning made of ground fresh red chiles. Asian markets carry the commercial product.

Shallots

Small, mild members of the onion family frequently used in Southeast Asia. Yellow or white onions may be substituted. One medium onion equals about 12 small shallots.

Shrimp chips

Called *krupuk* in Indonesia, these are hard discs of shrimp paste that become puffy when deep-fried. Chinese and Indonesian markets sell them. See instructions for frying on page 17.

Shrimp paste

Malays and Indonesians use this strong-smelling paste in many dishes. The flavor in the finished dish is much less intense than the aroma produced while the paste is cooked. The Malay name for the paste is *belacan* or *blachan*. The Indonesian name is *terasi*. Thai shrimp paste is called *kapi*.

Soybean condiment

A Chinese seasoning made of soybeans. It is brownish-yellow in color and may contain some portions of the whole bean.

Indonesian-style soy sauce

A dark, sweet, rich-tasting soy sauce that is used in Indonesian cookery. The Indonesian name is *kecap* (pronounced *ketjap*) *manis*.

Star anise

A hard, dark-brown, star-shaped spice. The flavor is related to licorice. Look for star anise in Chinese and other Oriental markets.

Tamarind

Tamarind pods contain pulp with a pleasant tart taste. The whole pods are sold in Latin and Asian markets. Blocks of peeled pulp, found in Indian and Asian stores, are more convenient to use. Liquid concentrate and powdered tamarind are also available. In the Philippines, green (unripe) tamarind is used to add tartness. Lemon juice may be substituted.

Thai tea
Orange-red tea leaves processed with vanilla flavoring to give a special flavor and color to the brewed tea.

Vinegars
Palm and sugar-cane vinegars are produced in the Philippines. Palm vinegar has a slight wine taste and cane vinegar a sweeter taste. Use the authentic vinegars if they are available. American distilled white vinegar is substituted in the Filipino dishes in this book. If desired, use unseasoned rice vinegar.

White radish
A large, long radish that is also known by its Japanese name, *daikon.*

Wrappers
A number of recipes call for wrapping the ingredients in pastry.

Egg-roll wrappers
Sheets of dough about 7 inches square are in the refrigerated section of Chinese markets and some supermarkets.

Lumpia wrappers
Thinner wrappers used for Filipino spring rolls. Chinese spring-roll or egg-roll wrappers may be substituted.

Won-ton wrappers
These miniature versions of Chinese egg-roll wrappers come in two shapes: square and round.

Young corn
Canned miniature ears of corn that are found in Chinese markets, gourmet stores and gourmet sections of supermarkets.

The Equipment
Asian cooking requires little special equipment. The most important tools are a wok, which can usually be replaced with a large skillet, and some means of grinding ingredients. A small capacity food processor is useful for grinding small batches of moist ingredients. An electric coffee grinder will grind dry spices to a powder. A mortar and pestle will also come in handy.

Basic Sauces & Seasonings

You can duplicate many Asian seasonings at home if the commercial product is not available.

Coconut Milk

Coconut milk is not the water inside the coconut but the rich white liquid that is squeezed from the grated coconut meat. Canned, frozen or powdered coconut milk or blocks of solid coconut cream can be substituted where grated fresh coconut is not available.

Southeast Asian cooks distinguish between coconut cream, also called *thick coconut milk,* which is squeezed without the addition of water, and the thinner milk produced by adding water to subsequent squeezings. These variations can be achieved by adjusting the amount of water added to powdered milk or solid coconut cream. If a can of coconut milk is not shaken, the thick coconut cream can be skimmed off the top.

When substituting homemade coconut milk for canned, remember that one 14-ounce can equals 1-3/4 cups coconut milk.

Fresh Coconut Milk

1 coconut

Preheat oven to 350F (175C). Pierce eyes of coconut and drain off water. Place coconut in a pie pan. Bake about 30 minutes or until shell cracks. Cool coconut until it can be handled. Tap all over with a hammer to crack shell further. Remove meat from shell. With a sharp knife, peel off brown skin. Cut meat into small dice. Place in a blender in batches; add hot tap water to the level of the coconut. Blend until finely grated, stopping blender occasionally and stirring if necessary. Pour coconut and liquid into a fine sieve placed over a medium bowl. Squeeze handfuls of coconut to extract as much liquid as possible. Return coconut to blender, add water to level of coconut and repeat blending and squeezing. Discard coconut. Add a dash of salt, cover and refrigerate until needed. Use within 1 day because fresh coconut milk will sour upon standing, or freeze up to 1 month.

One coconut yields 2 to 4 cups milk depending upon the richness desired.

Coconut Milk with Dried Coconut

Unsweetened dried coconut
Water

Unsweetened dried coconut is usually available in natural-food stores. Do not substitute sweetened dried coconut. Combine equal amounts by cups of dried coconut and hot water in a blender. Blend at high speed 30 seconds, turning blender on and off two or three times. Turn into a fine sieve placed over a medium bowl. Squeeze to extract as much milk as possible. For thinner milk, use twice as much water as coconut. Quantity of milk will be slightly less than amount of water added. Use within 1 day.

Rich Coconut Milk for Desserts

1 cup unsweetened dried coconut
1 cup water
1 cup evaporated milk

Combine coconut and water in a 1-quart saucepan. Bring to a boil, stirring. Remove from heat; let stand 10 to 15 minutes. Add milk; bring just to a boil. Remove from heat; let stand until cooled to room temperature. Place a fine sieve over a medium bowl. Pour mixture into sieve. Squeeze to extract as much liquid as possible. Cover and refrigerate if not using immediately. Use within 1 day. Makes 1-1/2 cups.

Clarified Butter

1 to 2 tablespoons more butter than
amount specified in recipe

Melt butter in a small heavy saucepan over medium heat. Spoon off white solids. Use only clear liquid butter.

Green Curry Paste
Gaeng Keo Wan (Thailand)

2 fresh green mild Anaheim-
chiles (about 1/4 lb.)
3 jalapeño chiles
1/4 cup loosely packed cilantro
leaves and stems
3 tablespoons finely sliced lemon
grass (1 stalk)
1/3 cup coarsely diced shallots
4 large garlic cloves
2 teaspoons Thai shrimp paste (kapi)
1 teaspoon black peppercorns
1 teaspoon ground dried galingal
1/2 teaspoon ground cumin
1/2 teaspoon ground turmeric
1/4 teaspoon salt
1 tablespoon oil

Place chiles on a baking sheet; broil until blistered all over. Place in a paper bag 15 minutes to steam. Peel. Discard stems and seeds. Combine all ingredients except oil in a small food processor fitted with the metal blade or in a blender; process as fine as possible. Stop processor or blender frequently to scrape down sides. Spoon mixture into a small jar or bowl;

stir in oil. Cover and refrigerate 1 day before using for flavors to blend. Refrigerate up to 1 week. Freeze for longer storage. Makes 3/4 cup.

Red Curry Paste
Gaeng Ped (Thailand)

7 hot dried red New Mexico chiles
10 small dried chiles
1/4 cup chopped shallots (2 large)
**3 tablespoons finely sliced lemon
  grass (1 stalk)**
**1 tablespoon chopped cilantro roots
  and stems**
**1 tablespoon Thai shrimp
  paste (kapi)**
3 large garlic cloves
**2 (1/8-inch-thick) slices thawed
  frozen galingal root or 1 teaspoon
  ground dried galingal**
**1 teaspoon chopped rehydrated dried
  kaffir lime peel or 1/2 teaspoon
  grated fresh lime peel**
1/2 teaspoon ground coriander
**1/2 teaspoon caraway seeds, ground
  in spice grinder**
1/4 teaspoon black pepper
1/4 teaspoon salt

Place chiles in a a large saucepan. Add water to cover; cover pan and bring to a boil. Remove from heat; let stand covered, 30 minutes or until chiles are soft. Drain chiles. Discard stems and seeds. Grind chiles very fine in a blender or food processor fitted with the metal blade, scraping down sides occasionally. Spoon into a sieve; force pulp through by pressing with the back of a spoon. Return pulp to blender or food processor. Add remaining ingredients. Process until pureed. Spoon into a small jar or bowl. Cover and refrigerate at least 1 day before using for flavors to blend. Refrigerate up to 2 weeks. Freeze for longer storage. Makes about 3/4 cup.

Variation

For a milder paste, use eight New Mexico-type chiles and eliminate the small chiles.

Crisp-Fried Onion Shreds
(Indonesia, Malaysia)

1 medium onion or 6 to 8 shallots
Oil for deep-frying

Cut onion or shallots in thin slices. Heat 2 inches oil in a small saucepan over medium heat. Add onion or shallot slices; fry until dry and golden brown. Do not burn. If onion browns too rapidly, reduce heat and cook more slowly. Drain on paper towels. Place in a small container; cover tightly until served. These are best served the same day as made. Exposure to air will cause shreds to wilt. Makes about 1 cup.

Roasted Peanuts
Raw unsalted shelled peanuts

Preheat oven to 350F (175C). Place peanuts in a single layer in a small baking pan. Bake 10 to 12 minutes or until browned. Shake pan occasionally; do not burn. Cool before using. In some recipes commercial dry-roasted unsalted peanuts can be substituted.

Fried Rice
(The Philippines)

2 tablespoons oil
1 garlic clove, minced
1-1/2 teaspoons chicken-bouillon
  granules
1 cup long-grain rice, cooked, cooled
2 green onions, minced
2 tablespoons shredded carrot
1 teaspoon Maggi seasoning

Heat a wok over medium heat. Add oil and heat. Add garlic; fry a few seconds. Stir in bouillon granules. Immediately add rice; stir to break up rice and mix with seasonings. Add onions, carrot and Maggi seasoning; cook, stirring, until rice is hot and evenly colored. Makes 4 servings.

Shrimp Chips
Krupuk Udang (Indonesia)

Shrimp-flavored chips
Oil for deep-frying

Heat 2 inches of oil in a wok or saucepan over medium heat. Add chips a few at a time. As soon as they puff up, remove and drain on paper towels. Serve immediately or store in an airtight container at room temperature a few days.

Sweet-Sour Dipping Sauce
Nuoc Cham Sauce (Vietnam)

1/2 cup rice vinegar
1/3 cup water
1/3 cup fish sauce
1/3 cup sugar
2 tablespoons long carrot shreds
1 tablespoon finely chopped fresh
  red chile or 1/2 teaspoon red-pepper
  flakes or 1/4 teaspoon red (cayenne)
  pepper
2 garlic cloves, minced

Combine rice vinegar, water, fish sauce and sugar in a small bowl. Stir until sugar dissolves. Add carrot, chile and garlic. Cover and let stand 1 hour to blend flavors. Serve at room temperature. Makes 1-1/4 cups.

Tamarind Liquid

1 to 2 tablespoons tamarind pulp
1/2 cup warm water

Combine tamarind pulp and water in a small bowl. Knead tamarind to extract color and flavor. Liquid will be cloudy and brown. Strain out seeds. Makes 1/2 cup.

Javanese Hot Sauce

Sambal Bajak (Indonesia)

1 red bell pepper
1 tablespoon oil
1/2 small onion, chopped
1 large garlic clove, minced
2 small fresh red chiles, seeded, chopped
1/4 lb. tomatoes, peeled, chopped
1 tablespoon dark-brown sugar
1-1/2 teaspoons fish sauce

Chop red pepper, discarding white membrane. Heat oil in a small saucepan. Add onion and garlic; sauté until tender. Add bell pepper, chiles and tomatoes. Cook until soft and juices from tomatoes have thickened. Remove from heat; cool. Turn into a small food processor fitted with the metal blade or a blender and purée. Return to saucepan. Add brown sugar and fish sauce. Bring to a boil; reduce heat and simmer a few moments, until thick and well blended. Remove from heat. Cool and store covered in refrigerator. Makes 1/2 cup.

Indonesian-Style Soy Sauce

Kecap Manis (Indonesia)

1/2 cup soy sauce
1/4 cup packed dark-brown sugar
3 tablespoons dark corn syrup
1 tablespoon molasses

Combine ingredients in a small bowl; stir until sugar dissolves. Pour into a small jar. Cover tightly and store at room temperature. This keeps almost indefinitely. Makes 3/4 cup.

Simple Syrup

1 cup sugar
1 cup water

Combine sugar and water in a small saucepan. Stir over medium heat until sugar dissolves. Bring to a full boil. Boil 3 minutes; cool. Store covered in refrigerator. Makes about 1-1/4 cups.

SINGAPOREAN SPREAD

When Singaporeans gather, food is often the most important topic of conversation. The island offers an immense variety of wonderful things to eat, including some of the same dishes you would find in neighboring Indonesia and Malaysia.

MENU

Straits Chinese Pork Satay

Chili Prawns

Fresh Rice Noodles with Beef

Fried Tofu

Steamed rice

Iced tea, beer or sangria

Fresh pineapple marinated in Grand Marnier
or pineapple sherbet

Straits Chinese Pork Satay
Satay Babi (Singapore)

Satay *is not only grilled but also fried
and stewed. An example of the latter is
this Straits Chinese recipe.*

1/2 lb. shallots or mild onions

6 candlenuts

**2 small dried hot chiles,
   stemmed, seeded**

1/2 teaspoon shrimp paste (terasi)

2 tablespoons oil

**1 lb. pork tenderloin, sliced
   1/4 inch thick**

1-1/4 cups coconut milk

2 tablespoons sugar

1 teaspoon salt

Steamed Rice

Combine shallots, candlenuts,
chiles and shrimp paste in a food
processor fitted with the metal
blade; process until puréed, stopping
processor and stirring down mixture
as needed. Heat oil in a 3-quart
saucepan over medium-high heat.
Add ground mixture; fry about 4
minutes, stirring often to keep from
burning. Add pork; cook 5 to 6
minutes or until no longer pink,
stirring frequently. Stir in coconut
milk, sugar and salt. Bring to a boil.
Reduce heat, cover and simmer 30
minutes, stirring occasionally. Serve
with rice. Makes 4 servings.

Chile Prawns
(Singapore)

Singaporeans are addicted to prawns (shrimp) or crab deluged with spicy sauce, and they consume great quantities on weekend excursions to the island's informal, open-air seafood restaurants.

1-1/4 lbs. medium shrimp

2 cups water

3 tablespoons finely chopped shallots (3 large)

2 large garlic cloves, minced

1 teaspoon minced gingerroot

1 small fresh green chile, minced

1/2 teaspoon hot chili powder

2 tablespoons tomato paste

1/2 teaspoon sugar

1/2 teaspoon salt

3 tablespoons oil

2 tablespoons beaten egg

Red chile flowers, shredded green onion or cilantro sprigs, if desired

Shell and devein shrimp, reserving 1 cup shrimp shells. Place shells in a medium saucepan. Add water and bring to a boil. Boil, uncovered, 15 minutes. Strain. There will be about 1 cup stock. In a small bowl, combine shallots, garlic, gingerroot, chile, chili powder, tomato paste, sugar and salt. Heat oil in a wok over high heat. Add shrimp and cook, stirring occasionally, until just pink, about 3 minutes. Lift carefully from wok to a plate, letting oil drain back into pan. Add shallot mixture; cook and stir over medium heat 2 minutes. Return shrimp to wok. Add 2/3 cup shrimp stock and cook over medium-high heat 2 minutes, stirring often. Stir in beaten egg; cook and stir until thickened slightly. Turn out onto a heated platter and garnish with red chile flowers and shredded green onion or cilantro, if desired. Makes 4 servings.

Fresh Steamed Rice Noodles with Beef

Beef Kway Teow (Singapore)

Many food stalls, or hawker stalls as they are called in Singapore, serve this dish. The fresh rice noodles are surprisingly sturdy and do not break up when stir-fried. If they are not available, try substituting an equal amount of cooked wide egg noodles.

1 lb. boneless lean beef steak (top sirloin, round steak or flank steak), sliced 1/8 inch thick

2 tablespoons soy sauce, divided

1 teaspoon oil

1/2 teaspoon salt

1/2 teaspoon sugar

1/4 cup oil

1 large shallot, thinly sliced

1 lb. fresh rice noodles

2 garlic cloves, minced

1/4 lb. bean sprouts

1/2 teaspoon cornstarch

2 tablespoons water

1 tablespoon oyster sauce

3 green onions, chopped

8 cilantro sprigs

Place steak in a medium bowl. Add 1 tablespoon of the soy sauce, 1 teaspoon oil, salt and sugar; mix well. Cover and marinate in refrigerator 1 hour or longer. Heat remaining 1/4 cup oil in a small skillet. Add shallot; fry until browned and crisp. Drain on paper towels; set aside for garnish. Reserve 3 tablespoons oil. If rice noodles are not pre-cut, cut into strips 1/2 inch wide. Heat a wok over medium-high heat. Add 2 tablespoons reserved oil and heat. Add 1/2 of the garlic; fry a few seconds. Add bean sprouts, then noodles and remaining 1 tablespoon soy sauce. Stir-fry 2 minutes. Spoon noodles onto a heated platter; keep warm. Do not wash wok. Mix cornstarch and water in a cup. Add remaining 1 tablespoon reserved oil to wok and heat. Add remaining garlic; fry a few seconds. Add steak; stir-fry 1-1/2 minutes. Add oyster sauce; stir-fry 30 seconds. Stir cornstarch mixture; add to wok and stir. Stir 30 seconds or until sauce is thickened. Place steak on top of noodles. Sprinkle with green onions, then fried shallot. Garnish with cilantro. Makes 4 servings.

Fried Tofu

Tahu Goreng (Indonesia)

Hot tofu, crunchy cold bean sprouts and lettuce make an interesting combination.

1/4 lb. bean sprouts, washed, drained

3 large iceberg-lettuce leaves, cut into 1/4-inch slices (2 cups)

1/2 cup oil

2 tablespoons raw peanuts

2 tofu slices (about 9-1/2 oz.) from a 19-oz. carton packed in slices

Soy-Sauce Dressing:

3 tablespoons mushroom soy sauce or regular soy sauce

2 tablespoons rice vinegar

2 tablespoons sugar

1 small garlic clove, minced

1/8 to 1/4 teaspoon hot red-pepper flakes

Mix bean sprouts and lettuce in a medium bowl. Cover and refrigerate. Prepare Soy-Sauce Dressing. Heat oil in a small saucepan to 375F (190C.) Add peanuts; fry until browned, being careful not to burn. Remove with a slotted spoon; drain on paper towels. Cool; reserve oil. Crush peanuts in a mortar or with a rolling pin; set aside. Just before serving, remove tofu from container. Cut each slice in half through the side to make 4 thinner slices of the same size. Cut these slices in half crosswise, making 8 tofu slices. Reheat oil in saucepan. Fry tofu slices 2 or 3 at a time until lightly browned and puffy. Drain on paper towels; keep warm. To serve, mound lettuce mixture on a platter. Sprinkle with Soy-Sauce Dressing. Place fried tofu around edges of salad. Sprinkle crushed peanuts over all. Makes 4 servings.

Soy-Sauce Dressing:
Combine all ingredients in a small bowl; let stand 30 minutes or longer to blend flavors. Makes 1/3 cup.

Hari Raya Buffet

I n Muslim countries like Malaysia, Indonesia and Brunei, the fasting month of Ramadan ends with Hari Raya, a holiday marked by feasting, open houses and the wearing of ornate traditional costumes. Family members gather from far points to enjoy the celebration together, collaborating in the preparation of elaborate meals like this.

MENU

Fish with Spicy Tamarind Sauce

Beef in Ginger-Tomato Sauce

Raffles Lamb Curry or Lamb Satay, page 69

Dry Vegetable Curry with Cilantro

Aromatic Steamed Rice

Penang Papaya Pudding

Assorted small cakes and cookies

Fruit juices

Tea and coffee

Fish with Spicy Tamarind Sauce

Ikan Sambal (Brunei)

The sauce can be prepared in advance and reheated, reducing last-minute work to the frying of the fish.

1 lb. lean white fish fillets

1 teaspoon ground turmeric

1/4 teaspoon salt

3 tablespoons oil

1 thin slice from a medium onion, separated into rings

Tamarind Sauce:

8 shallots or 1/2 medium onion

2 large garlic cloves

1 small fresh red chile, chopped

1/2 teaspoon shrimp paste (terasi), if desired

1 tablespoon oil

1/2 cup Tamarind Liquid, page 18

1-1/2 teaspoons sugar

1/2 teaspoon salt

Cut fish into 4 portions. Rub turmeric over both sides of each fillet. Sprinkle with salt. Cover and refrigerate. Make Tamarind Sauce. Heat oil in a skillet large enough to hold fish in a single layer. Add fish; fry 2-1/2 to 3 minutes on each side, depending upon thickness, or until fish has turned from translucent to opaque when tested with a fork. Place fish on a heated platter. Spoon sauce over fish. Garnish with onion rings; keep warm. Makes 4 servings.

Tamarind Sauce:
Combine shallots, garlic, chile and shrimp paste, if desired, in a blender or food processor fitted with the metal blade; process until very fine. Heat oil in a small saucepan. Add ground mixture; sauté gently 3 minutes. Add Tamarind Liquid, sugar and salt. Bring to a boil. Reduce heat; simmer gently, uncovered, 5 minutes or until thickened, stirring frequently; keep warm. Makes 1/2 cup.

Beef in Ginger-Tomato Sauce

Beef Jaal Frezy (Malaysia)

Pakistani in origin, this spicy beef dish from Kuala Lumpur resembles a Chinese stir-fry.

**1 lb. trimmed beef steak (top
    sirloin), 1/2 to 3/4 inch thick,
    partially frozen**

2 tablespoons oil

1 large onion, chopped

**1 (1-1/2-inch-thick) gingerroot
    piece, minced**

4 large garlic cloves, minced

**2 medium tomatoes (1/2 lb.),
    chopped**

1-1/2 teaspoons ground coriander

1 teaspoon sugar

1 teaspoon salt

1/4 teaspoon red (cayenne) pepper

1/8 teaspoon black pepper

**1/4 cup lightly
    packed cilantro leaves**

Cut beef into 1/8-inch-thick slices; set aside. Heat oil in a large skillet over medium heat. Add onion; cook, stirring often, until onion starts to brown. Add gingerroot and garlic; cook 3 minutes, stirring to prevent burning. Increase heat, add beef and cook until browned, about 5 minutes, stirring to mix with seasonings. Stir in tomatoes; cook 3 minutes or until blended with sauce. Stir in coriander, sugar, salt, red pepper and black pepper. Reduce heat, cover and simmer 3 minutes. Uncover and stir in cilantro. Makes 4 servings.

Raffles Lamb Curry

Kari Kambing (Singapore)

Serve the curry with rice, mango chutney and assorted curry condiments.

2 tablespoons curry powder

2 tablespoons water

2 tablespoons oil

1 tablespoon minced gingerroot

3 large garlic cloves, minced

2 lbs. boneless lean lamb, cut into
  1-inch cubes

1 cup water

1/2 cup evaporated milk

1/4 cup canned tomato puree

1 (1-inch) cinnamon stick

4 green cardamom pods

4 whole cloves

1-1/2 teaspoons salt

Dash black pepper

Suggested condiments:
Fresh or dried shredded coconut,
raisins, toasted peanuts, chopped
hard-cooked egg, diced tomato,
sliced banana

Blend curry powder and water in a small bowl to form a soft paste. Heat oil in a Dutch oven over medium heat. Add curry paste, gingerroot and garlic; fry 2 minutes, stirring to keep from burning. Increase heat, add meat and cook until no longer pink, about 8 minutes, stirring often to mix with seasonings. Add remaining ingredients. Bring to a boil. Reduce heat, cover and simmer 45 minutes or until meat is tender. Makes 6 servings.

▲ *One evening I went to a lane in Kuala Lumpur lined with food stalls. There were lots of customers, and the tables were loaded with steaming dishes. Conversation was lively, but nobody touched the food, which puzzled me. Then, suddenly, everyone began to eat. It turned out to be Ramadan. The sun had just set, ending the daily fast until sunrise the next morning.*

Dry Vegetable Curry with Cilantro

Nentara (Singapore)

Lively Indian-style dishes are part of the mixed heritage of Singapore and Malaysia.

1 mild green Anaheim-type chile

1/4 lb. small whole boiling onions

2 tablespoons Clarified Butter,
  page 15, or oil

1/2 teaspoon cumin seeds

3/4 teaspoon salt

1/4 teaspoon ground turmeric

Dash red (cayenne) pepper

1 tablespoon shredded gingerroot

1/2 lb. cauliflower, cut into small
  flowerets

1 (8-oz.) russet potato, peeled, cut
  into 1-inch chunks, in cold water

2 tablespoons water

3/4 cup thawed frozen peas

1 large tomato, unpeeled, cut into
  3/4-inch chunks

1/2 teaspoon garam masala

1 cup lightly packed cilantro leaves,
  chopped

Broil chile until blistered all over. Peel and cut into thin strips 1-1/2 to 2 inches long. Cut onions into halves or quarters if large. Heat butter or oil in a deep skillet over medium heat. Add cumin seeds; fry 30 seconds, stirring. Stir in salt, turmeric and red pepper. Add gingerroot, chili strips, onions, cauliflowerets and drained potato. Gently stir until vegetables are coated with seasonings. Add 1 tablespoon water. Reduce heat, cover and simmer 15 minutes. If too dry, add 1 tablespoon water. Add peas and tomato. Sprinkle with garam masala. Cover and cook 5 minutes. Just before serving, gently stir in cilantro. Turn into a heated serving bowl. Makes 4 to 6 servings.

Aromatic Steamed Rice

Nasi Biryani (Malaysia)

Clarified butter, a substitute for Indian ghee, adds richness to rice, but oil may be used. The last-minute addition of turmeric produces splashes of color. It's a replacement for costly saffron.

1 cup basmati rice or other long-grain rice

1/4 cup oil

1 small onion, halved through stem end, thinly sliced

3 tablespoons Clarified Butter, page 15

1 (2-inch) cinnamon stick

4 green cardamom pods

4 whole cloves

6 black peppercorns

1 garlic clove, minced

1-3/4 cups chicken broth

1 teaspoon salt

3/4 teaspoon ground turmeric

1 tablespoon water

Wash rice thoroughly. Soak 1 hour in water to cover. Drain well. Heat oil in a small skillet. Add 1/3 of the onion slices; fry until browned. Drain on paper towel and set aside. Heat 2 tablespoons butter in a heavy 3-quart saucepan. Add cinnamon stick, cardamom pods, cloves and peppercorns; fry 30 seconds. Add garlic and remaining onion; cook until onion is tender. Add rice and cook 2 minutes, stirring frequently. Add broth and salt. Cover and boil until broth is absorbed, about 10 minutes. Reduce heat to very low and steam, covered, 30 minutes. Use a heat diffuser if necessary to prevent rice from sticking and burning. Pour remaining 1 tablespoon butter over rice. Blend turmeric with water in a small cup and drizzle over top of rice. Cover and steam 10 minutes. Fluff lightly with fork, but do not blend turmeric evenly with rice. Color should be irregular. Spoon into a heated serving dish. Sprinkle with reserved fried onion. Makes 4 to 6 servings.

Penang Papaya Pudding
Puding Betik (Malaysia)

This papaya-orange dessert makes a light and elegant ending to a meal, no matter what its nationality.

1 (1-1/2-lb.) papaya
1/2 cup sugar
3 tablespoons cornstarch
Dash salt
1 cup orange juice
2 tablespoons lemon juice
2 strawberries, halved, or
  4 raspberries
4 mint leaves

Cut papaya in half; scoop out seeds. Cut papaya into wedges; peel. Process papaya until pureed in a blender or food processor fitted with the metal blade; there should be about 1-1/4 cups. Combine sugar, cornstarch and salt in a 1-quart saucepan. Gradually stir in orange juice. Add papaya puree and lemon juice. Cook over medium heat, stirring constantly, until mixture boils and thickens enough to separate slightly when spoon is drawn across the pan. Spoon into a bowl, cover and refrigerate until chilled. Just before serving, stir well. Spoon into stemmed dessert glasses. Garnish each serving with a strawberry half or a raspberry and a mint leaf. Makes 4 servings.

▲ *Penang is an island off the west coast of Maylasia, with a large Chinese population. A young charming Chinese lady from Penang prepared this dessert for me.*

Three-Course Thai Dinner

You would not expect to find sugar in noodles, or onions in dessert, but these unorthodox Thai combinations are surprisingly good.

MENU

Hot & Sour Beef Salad

Stir-Fried Steamed Rice Noodles

Sweet-Potato Custard with Fried Shallots

Hot & Sour Beef Salad

Yam Nua (Thailand)

A little meat, a lot of vegetables and an oil-free dressing add up to a healthful dish. This salad is widely served in Bangkok and at Thai restaurants in the United States.

1/2 cup lime juice

3 tablespoons sugar

2 tablespoons fish sauce

3 small fresh green chiles, thinly sliced

6 large romaine-lettuce leaves

1 small cucumber, peeled, sliced, 1/8 inch thick

2 small tomatoes, each cut into 8 wedges

1 small red onion (1/4 lb.), halved, thinly sliced

1 (1- to 1-1/4-lb.) flank steak

1 teaspoon garlic salt

3 large green onions, including some of the tops, sliced

1/2 cup cilantro sprigs

Combine lime juice, sugar, fish sauce and chiles in a small bowl. Cover and let stand 1 hour. Cut lettuce crosswise into slices 1/2 inch wide. Arrange lettuce on a platter. Arrange cucumber slices at each end and tomatoes at sides. Scatter onion over top. Cover and refrigerate platter until chilled. Sprinkle meat with garlic salt. Let stand 30 to 45 minutes. Preheat broiler. Place steak on rack in a broiler pan. Broil 4 inches from heat source 5 minutes; turn and broil 3 more minutes. Steak will be rare; adjust cooking time according to thickness. Cut steak across the grain into 1/4-inch-thick slices. Cut very long slices in half. Arrange steak slices on lettuce. Top with green onions and cilantro sprigs. Spoon dressing over salad. Makes 4 servings.

Stir-Fried Rice Noodles

Pad Thai (Thailand)

Sweet-sour seasonings, crisp bean sprouts and crunchy peanuts in the noodles make this a memorable dish.

**1/2 lb. (1/8-inch-wide) dried
  rice noodles**

**1 whole chicken breast, boned,
  skinned**

8 medium shrimp, shelled, deveined

1/2 cup water

1/4 cup fish sauce

3 tablespoons sugar

1 tablespoon lime juice

1 teaspoon paprika

1/8 teaspoon red (cayenne) pepper

1/2 lb. bean sprouts

**3 green onions, white part only, cut
  into 1-inch shreds**

3 tablespoons oil

4 large garlic cloves, finely chopped

1 egg

**4 tablespoons finely crushed
  Roasted Peanuts, page 17**

Place rice noodles in a large bowl. Cover with water; soak 45 minutes. Cut chicken into 1-1/2 x 1/3-inch strips. Cut shrimp in half lengthwise; set aside. Combine water, fish sauce, sugar, lime juice, paprika and red pepper in a small bowl; set aside. Reserve 1/4 of the bean sprouts for topping; combine remaining bean sprouts and green onions. Drain noodles. Heat a wok over medium-high heat. Add oil and heat. Add garlic; fry until garlic starts to brown. Increase heat. Add chicken; stir-fry until almost cooked, about 2 minutes. Push chicken to 1 side. Break egg into wok. Stir quickly to break up yolk and scramble egg. When egg is set, mix with chicken. Add drained noodles, shrimp, fish-sauce mixture and 3 tablespoons peanuts. Cook and stir over high heat 2 to 3 minutes or until noodles are soft and most of liquid is absorbed. Add green-onion mixture; cook, stirring, 1 minute longer. Spoon onto a heated platter. Sprinkle with reserved bean sprouts and peanuts. Makes 6 servings.

Sweet-Potato Custard with Fried Shallots

Khanom Mo Ken (Thailand)

The idea may sound odd, but crisp-fried shallots scattered over the top are a wonderful complement to this dessert.

1-1/2 cups coconut milk
3 eggs
1/3 cup packed dark-brown sugar
1/3 cup packed light-brown sugar
1/2 cup mashed boiled sweet potato
1/8 teaspoon salt
1/4 cup oil
6 small shallots, very thinly sliced

Preheat oven to 350F (175C). Combine coconut milk, eggs, brown sugars, sweet potato and salt in a blender; blend thoroughly. Butter a 1-quart heat-proof baking dish. Pour mixture into dish. Set in a large baking pan; add hot water to come halfway up sides of dish. Bake 50 minutes or until a knife inserted off-center of custard comes out clean. Remove from hot water. Preheat broiler. Place custard so top is about 4 inches from heat source. Broil custard 1-1/2 to 2 minutes or until top is browned; set aside. Heat oil in a small skillet. Add shallots; fry until browned and crisp. Drain on paper towels. Scatter shallots over top of pudding. Serve warm or at room temperature. Makes 6 servings.

Variation
Substitute mashed boiled taro or pumpkin for the sweet potato.

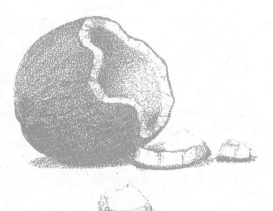

Shrimp for Supper

The spread of shrimp farming has made this once-luxury shellfish more widely available and reasonable in price. Malaysia, one of the Southeast Asian nations contributing to this abundance, is the source of the colorful main dish.

MENU
Shrimp in Tomato Sauce

Asparagus with Red Curry Paste

Sweet & Sour Green-Bean Relish

Baked Yellow Rice

Coconut Ice Cream

Shrimp in Tomato Sauce

Sambal Udang *(Malaysia)*

This shrimp dish from Kuala Lumpur would be one of several dishes served with rice at a Malay meal.

2 tablespoons oil
1/2 medium onion, finely chopped
2 shallots, finely chopped
2 garlic cloves, minced
1-1/2 teaspoons minced gingerroot
1/2 teaspoon sambal velek or
  1 small fresh red chile, sliced,
  or dash red (cayenne) pepper
2 tablespoons tomato sauce
1 tablespoon tomato paste
1 teaspoon sugar
3/4 teaspoon salt
1/8 teaspoon shrimp paste (terasi),
  if desired
1/4 cup water
1 lb. medium shrimp, shelled,
  deveined
4 cilantro sprigs

Heat oil in a medium skillet. Add onion, shallots, garlic, gingerroot and sambal velek, chile or red pepper; cook, stirring, until onion is tender. Stir in tomato sauce, tomato paste, sugar, salt, shrimp paste, if desired, and water; simmer until shrimp paste is dissolved and mixture is hot. Add shrimp; cook over medium-high heat 4 minutes or just until shrimp turn pink, stirring often. Spoon into a heated serving dish; garnish with cilantro sprigs. Makes 4 servings.

▲ *In Bali, I've had superb shrimp-and-avocado salads. And in Singapore, Indonesia and Malaysia, it's routine to toss a few shrimp into a noodle dish along with shredded meat and tofu.*

There's shrimp satay too, and the Thai hot and sour shrimp soup—Tom Yum Goong—is as popular in Malaysia as in Thailand. Food stalls in Kota Bahru near the Thai border sometimes add rice or noodles to the broth.

Asparagus with Red Curry Paste
Pad Prik King (Thailand)

Thinly sliced asparagus cooks in record time. Green beans are a year-round alternative, try both.

3/4 lb. asparagus or green beans
1 tablespoon oil
1-1/2 teaspoons Red Curry Paste,
  page 16
1 tablespoon fish sauce
1 tablespoon water
1/4 teaspoon black pepper

Snap off tough ends of asparagus stalks. Cut asparagus diagonally into slices about 1/8 inch thick. If using green beans, snap off ends. Cut diagonally into 1-inch pieces. Cook green beans in boiling salted water in a medium saucepan 3 minutes or until crisp-tender; drain. Do not precook asparagus. Heat a wok over medium-high heat. Add oil and heat. Stir in curry paste. Add asparagus or green beans; stir-fry 1 minute. Add fish sauce, water and pepper; stir-fry 1 minute. Spoon onto a heated platter. Makes 4 servings.

Variation
These vegetables will be very spicy. For a milder flavor, use 1/2 to 1 teaspoon curry paste and 1/8 teaspoon black pepper.

Sweet & Sour Green-Bean Relish

Acar Buncis (Indonesia)

These sweet-and-sour beans would fit an American potluck as easily as an Indonesian dinner.

1/2 lb. green beans
1/2 cup water
2 tablespoons sugar
1 teaspoon salt
1/2 teaspoon garlic salt
2 tablespoons white vinegar
1/4 cup chopped red onion

Snap ends off beans. Cut diagonally into slices about 1 inch long and 1/4 inch wide at widest part. Place beans, water, sugar, salt and garlic salt in a 1-quart saucepan. Bring to a boil. Reduce heat. Cover and simmer 10 to 12 minutes, or until just tender. Stir in vinegar. Spoon into a serving bowl. Sprinkle onion over top. Cover and refrigerate at least 2 hours before serving. Makes about 6 servings.

Baked Yellow Rice

Nasi Kuning (Singapore)

Adapted from traditional recipes, this is an easy way to prepare rice.

1 cup long-grain rice, washed, drained

1 tablespoon butter

1 teaspoon salt

1 teaspoon curry powder

1/2 teaspoon ground turmeric

2 cups boiling water

Preheat oven to 375F (190C). Place rice in an ungreased 1-1/2-quart baking dish. Add butter, salt, curry powder and turmeric. Add boiling water; stir until butter melts. Cover tightly; bake 25 minutes or until water is absorbed. Let stand, covered, 5 minutes before serving. Fluff with a fork before serving. Makes 4 servings.

Coconut Ice Cream

Ice Krem Kati (Thailand)

To serve the ice cream Thai-style, top it with cooked or canned corn kernels, roasted peanuts or both.

1 (1-pint) carton whipping cream (2 cups)

1 (14-oz.) can coconut milk (1-3/4 cups)

1/2 cup sugar

1 teaspoon coconut extract

1/8 teaspoon salt

Combine ingredients in an ice-cream-freezer container. Process according to manufacturer's instructions. Makes about 5 cups.

▲ *Coconut ice cream in Thailand is so creamy and natural tasting that I fell in love with it at once and took every opportunity to buy little cups of this luscious frozen treat from snack shops and supermarkets.*

Light Food for Light Eaters

This menu saves calories without sacrificing flavor. In typical Thai fashion, meat is combined with fresh herbs and raw vegetables.

MENU

Ground Turkey with Basil or Chicken Wrapped in Lettuce

Assorted raw vegetables with a light mayonnaise-based dip

Sesame crackers or steamed rice

Grapefruit or other fruit sorbet

Ground Turkey with Basil

Gai Nuong Pad Bai Horapha (Thailand)

When you need a quick, easy dish, try this. To vary the flavor, use beef or pork instead of turkey. Fresh basil is essential to this dish.

1 tablespoon oil

3 large garlic cloves, minced

1 fresh green chile, minced

3/4 lb. ground or chopped
  turkey breast

2 tablespoons soy sauce or
  fish sauce

1 teaspoon sugar

1 cup lightly packed basil leaves

Heat oil in a medium skillet. Add garlic and chile; cook 30 seconds. Add turkey; cook 2 minutes or until browned, stirring to break up turkey. Add soy sauce or fish sauce and sugar; cook 2 minutes. Add basil; cook, stirring, 1-1/2 minutes longer. Spoon onto a heated platter. Makes 4 servings.

Chicken Wrapped in Lettuce
Larb Gai (Thailand)

These savory little bundles will please light eaters.

2 tablespoons soy sauce

1 tablespoon fish sauce

2 teaspoons lemon juice

1 teaspoon water

1-1/2 teaspoons sugar

Scant 1/2 teaspoon black pepper

2 tablespoons oil

2 large garlic cloves, minced

2 whole chicken breasts, boned, skinned, cut into 1/2-inch chunks

1/2 medium onion, thinly sliced

1 small or 1/2 large red bell pepper, slivered

2 small fresh green chiles, sliced lengthwise

1/4 cup lightly packed mint leaves

8 butter-lettuce or other leaf-lettuce leaves

Combine soy sauce, fish sauce, lemon juice, water, sugar and pepper in a small bowl; set aside. Heat wok over high heat. Add oil and heat. Add garlic; stir-fry 30 seconds. Add chicken and onion; stir-fry 1 minute. Add bell pepper and chiles; stir-fry 2 minutes. Add soy-sauce mixture; cook, stirring, 30 seconds. Stir in mint; cook 20 seconds. Spoon onto a heated platter. To eat, tear lettuce leaves into pieces, spoon some of the chicken mixture onto each piece, wrap and eat. Makes 4 servings.

Salad Buffet by the Pool

On a very hot day, offer glasses of fresh limeade made Thai-style, with a dash of salt as well as sugar.

MENU
Mango Margarita
Festival Chicken Salad
Bean-Thread Salad with Chicken & Shrimp
Galloping Horses
Bangkok-Style Steak Salad
Hot muffins, cornbread wedges
Mixed Fruits with Grass Jelly & Ice
Iced tea, limeade, fruit juice

Mango Margarita

(Brunei)

A big, frosty drink—lovely for summer parties.

1/2 mango, peeled, seeded
3 oz. (6 tablespoons) tequila
1 oz. (2 tablespoons) triple sec
1-1/2 oz. (3 tablespoons) lime juice
3/4 oz. (1-1/2 tablespoons) Simple
  Syrup, page 18
6 ice cubes

Combine all ingredients in a blender; blend until slushy. Makes 1 large or 2 medium servings.

▲ *Thanks to tourist demand, Mexican food is thriving in Southeast Asia. I've had excellent enchiladas in Singapore, tacos in Bangkok, great guacamole and nachos in Bali. This Margarita, served at the Sheraton Utama hotel in Bandar Seri Begawan, the capital of Brunei, also comes in a non-alcoholic version for Muslims.*

Festival Chicken Salad

Naum Gai (Thailand)

The Thai cook who prepared this salad for a temple festival suggested steamed rice as an accompaniment. Use small or medium chicken breasts.

2 small whole chicken breasts, boned, skinned

1/2 teaspoon salt

3 green onions, including a little of the tops, chopped

1/4 cup lightly packed cilantro leaves, chopped

Romaine or other leafy lettuce

4 whole green onions

4 cherry tomatoes

1 cup bean sprouts

Festival Dressing:
1/3 cup lemon juice

4 teaspoons fish sauce

1 garlic clove, minced

3/4 teaspoon salt

1/2 teaspoon hot red-pepper flakes

Put chicken through the medium blade of a meat grinder or process in a food processor fitted with the metal blade. Bring 6 cups water and salt to a boil in a 3-quart saucepan. Add chicken, stirring to break up. Boil 2 minutes or until chicken is white and cooked through. Drain thoroughly; cool. Make Festival Dressing. Place chicken in a medium bowl. Add dressing, chopped green onions and cilantro. Toss to combine. Cover and refrigerate until chilled. Line a platter or individual plates with lettuce leaves. Spoon salad over lettuce. Garnish with whole green onions, cherry tomatoes and bean sprouts. Makes 4 servings.

Festival Dressing:
Stir ingredients in a small bowl until salt dissolves.

Bean-Thread Salad with Chicken & Shrimp

Yam Woon Sen (Thailand)

Unlike other forms of pasta, bean-thread noodles become transparent when cooked. The golden needles and black fungus, added for crunchy texture, are dried ingredients available in Chinese shops.

18 medium shrimp, shelled, deveined, cooked

1 chicken-breast half, cooked, shredded

1/4 cup dried golden needles

2 small pieces dried black fungus

2-1/2 oz. bean-thread noodles

3 tablespoons sliced green-onion tops

1/4 cup lightly packed cilantro leaves

1 teaspoon finely chopped mint

3 or 4 romaine-lettuce leaves

2 tablespoons unsalted Roasted Peanuts, page 17, chopped

6 cilantro springs

Lemon Dressing:

1/3 cup lemon juice

3 tablespoons fish sauce

4 teaspoons sugar

2 garlic cloves, minced

1 small fresh green chile, sliced crosswise

Dash white pepper

Cover and refrigerate shrimp and chicken. Separately soak golden needles, black fungus and bean-thread noodles in water about 30 minutes or until soft. Drain, rinse and squeeze golden needles to extract excess water. Drain, rinse and cut black fungus into fine shreds. Bring 8 cups water to a boil in a saucepan. Drain bean threads, add to boiling water and boil 3 minutes until transparent. Drain; cut to shorter lengths. Cool. Make Lemon Dressing. Combine shrimp, chicken, golden needles, black fungus, green-onion tops, cilantro leaves and mint in a large bowl. Add Lemon Dressing; toss to combine. Add bean threads; toss. Cover and refrigerate. Line a platter with lettuce leaves. Set aside 1 teaspoon chopped peanuts. Toss remainder with salad. Arrange salad on lettuce. Sprinkle with peanuts; garnish with cilantro sprigs. Makes 6 servings.

Lemon Dressing:
Combine all ingredients in a small bowl; stir until sugar dissolves.

Galloping Horses

Ma Ho (Thailand)

Fresh pineapple is the foundation of this refreshing and unusual salad. As a variation, substitute orange slices for the pineapple.

1/2 pineapple (halved lengthwise)
2 tablespoons oil
1 tablespoon raw peanuts
1 garlic clove, minced
1/4 lb. boneless lean pork, finely ground
1 tablespoon fish sauce or soy sauce
1 tablespoon sugar
1/2 teaspoon white vinegar
1/4 cup cilantro leaves
1 small fresh red chile, slivered

Cut pineapple half lengthwise in 2 equal pieces. Remove core; peel and remove eyes. Cut pineapple crosswise into slices 1/4 to 1/3 inch thick. Overlap slices on a platter; set aside. Heat oil in a small skillet. Add peanuts; fry until browned. Remove skillet from heat. Remove peanuts, reserving oil. Coarsely crush peanuts in a mortar or with a rolling pin. Reheat oil over medium heat. Add garlic; fry a few seconds. Increase heat, add pork and cook until no longer pink, stirring to break up meat. Stir in peanuts, fish sauce, sugar and vinegar. Cook until most of liquid has boiled away but pork is still moist; do not overcook or meat will be dry. Spoon pork over pineapple slices. Arrange cilantro over pork. Decorate with chile slivers. Serve at room temperature. Makes 4 servings.

Bangkok-Style Steak Salad

Yam Nua (Thailand)

A creamy, herb-flavored ranch-type dressing from the supermarket will produce good results with this recipe.

1 bunch cilantro, rinsed

3 medium garlic cloves

1 teaspoon black peppercorns

1 tablespoon soy sauce

1-1/2 teaspoons Worcestershire sauce

1 (1-lb.) flank steak

2 tablespoons oil

6 large butter-lettuce or
   red-leaf-lettuce leaves

1/2 cup thinly sliced red onion (cut
   slices into thirds or quarters before
   measuring)

1/3 cucumber, peeled, thinly sliced

1 medium tomato, halved, cored,
   sliced

1/3 cup bottled non-sweet, creamy,
   ranch-type dressing

Cut off any roots and a small portion of cilantro stems; there should be about 2 tablespoons, loosely packed. Place cilantro roots and stems, garlic and peppercorns in a mortar; pound until reduced to a paste. Stir in soy sauce and Worcestershire sauce. Rub mixture over both sides of steak. Place steak in a shallow dish. Cover and marinate in refrigerator 4 to 6 hours. Heat oil in a medium, preferably non-stick, skillet over medium-high heat. Skillet should be large enough to hold steak flat. Add steak. Cover and cook 4 minutes. Turn, cover and cook second side 4 minutes. Steak will be medium rare. Remove to a cutting board. Cool slightly, then cut across the grain into slices about 1/3 inch thick and 1-1/2 to 2 inches long, reserving juices. Cool to room temperature. Meanwhile, wash lettuce; tear into bite-size pieces. Place in a salad bowl. Add onion, cucumber and tomato; toss lightly with dressing. Add sliced steak and steak juices; toss to mix. Makes 4 servings.

Mixed Fruits with Grass Jelly & Ice

Es Shanghai (Indonesia)

This hot-weather cooler is a cross between a dessert and a drink. As the ice melts, it turns into a beverage. After eating the fruits and jelly, drink or spoon up the remaining liquid.

1 cup water

2/3 cup sugar

1 teaspoon vanilla extract

1/2 teaspoon red food color

1/2 cup diced fresh or canned mango, drained

1/2 cup diced canned pineapple, drained

2 cups diced Chinese grass jelly

24 canned palm seeds

4 cups finely crushed ice

1/2 cup whipping cream

1/2 cup milk

Combine water and sugar in a small saucepan. Bring to a boil, stirring just until sugar is dissolved. Boil 1 minute. Remove from heat. Stir in vanilla and food color. Cool slightly, cover and refrigerate until chilled. In each of 4 large wine glasses or other large stemmed glasses, place 2 tablespoons mango, 2 tablespoons pineapple, 1/2 cup grass jelly and 6 palm seeds. Top with 1 cup crushed ice. Mix whipping cream and milk. Pour 1/4 cup mixture over each serving. Top with 1/4 cup vanilla syrup. Serve at once. Makes 4 servings.

Variation
Instead of grass jelly, use cubes of firm gelatin in any flavor. Canned lychees, fresh grapes or other fruit may be substituted for palm seeds. Lychees are large so reduce quantity to 3 per serving.

Seashore Dinner

Asians relish huge meals composed of one seafood dish after another. This menu is modest compared to what might be served at a seafood restaurant in Bangkok or Singapore.

MENU

Squid with Hot Wine Sauce

Fish with Pineapple & Tamarind

Lemony Shrimp

Steamed crab claws

Noodles with Shrimp, Pork & Vegetables

*Stir-fried bok choy, kangkong or other
leafy green vegetable*

*Lychee-Pineapple Dessert or plate of
fresh orange wedges*

Squid with Hot Wine Sauce
Pla Mueg Pad Prik (Thailand)

Do not overcook squid or it will become chewy and tough. In this recipe, tender small squid are scored Chinese-style, sliced and cooked just 3 minutes. The recipe, from Bangkok, is an interesting blend of Asian ingredients including Chinese oyster sauce, Thai fish sauce and Chinese or Japanese rice wine.

2 lbs. small squid (3 to 4 inches long)

1/3 cup rice wine

2 tablespoons fish sauce

1 tablespoon oyster sauce

1/2 teaspoon sugar

Dash white pepper

3 tablespoons oil

8 shallots, sliced

3 large garlic cloves, sliced

4 green onions, white part only, sliced

2 small fresh red chiles, sliced

1/4 cup lightly packed cilantro leaves, chopped

Clean squid. Pull out and discard all contents of the hood; rinse well. Discard tentacles. Under running water, pull off the thin speckled peel that coats the hood. Slit each squid lengthwise down 1 side and open flat. Make diagonal slashes across squid in 1 direction about 1/2 inch apart, being careful not to cut through squid. Now make diagonal slashes in opposite direction, forming diamonds. Squid may be prepared in advance to this state, then covered and refrigerated a few hours. Combine rice wine, fish sauce, oyster sauce, sugar and pepper. Heat wok over high heat. Add oil and heat. Add shallots and garlic; cook until lightly browned. Add squid, green onions, chiles and wine mixture. Cook, stirring often, 3 minutes. Stir in chopped cilantro. Serve at once. Makes 4 servings.

Fish with Pineapple & Tamarind

Ikan Asam (Singapore)

Distinctive Straits Chinese seasonings blend in this dish. The pineapple should be very sweet to give the proper flavor. For spicy authenticity, double the amount of chiles.

1 small dried chile

2 rounded tablespoons tamarind
  pulp

1-1/2 cups warm water

1 small fresh green chile, sliced

1/2 lb. shallots or 2 small onions

6 candlenuts

1 teaspoon shrimp paste (terasi)

1 teaspoon ground dried galingal

1/2 teaspoon ground turmeric

2 tablespoons oil

1-1/2 cups warm water

2-1/2 tablespoons sugar

2 teaspoons salt

1 lemon-grass stalk, pounded

1 cup fresh pineapple chunks
  (1/4 medium pineapple)

1-1/2 lbs. red snapper fillets

Soak dried chile in warm water until softened; drain. Discard stem and seeds. Combine tamarind and 1-1/2 cups warm water in a medium bowl. Knead tamarind to extract flavor and color. Strain liquid into a small bowl, discarding pulp; set aside. Combine dried and fresh chiles, shallots, candlenuts, shrimp paste, galingal and turmeric in a blender or food processor fitted with the metal blade; process to a paste. Heat oil in a large skillet over medium heat. Add ground mixture; sauté 5 minutes, stirring to prevent burning. Add tamarind liquid, remaining 1-1/2 cups water, sugar, salt, lemon grass and pineapple. Bring to a boil, reduce heat and simmer 3 minutes. If desired, prepare in advance to this point, then reheat before adding fish. Lay fish fillets in sauce. Bring to a boil again. Reduce heat; simmer, uncovered, 10 minutes, or until fish has turned from translucent to opaque when tested with a fork. Remove lemon grass. Serve with rice to soak up the sauce. Makes 4 servings.

Lemony Shrimp

Goong Pla (Thailand)

The shrimp are cooked separately, then tossed with shallots, lemon grass, onions and a lemony dressing.

2 garlic cloves

2 small fresh green chiles, sliced

3 tablespoons lemon juice

1 tablespoon fish sauce

1 tablespoon soy sauce

1 teaspoon Maggi seasoning

1 lb. medium shrimp

6 large shallots or 1 small onion, thinly sliced, (about 1 cup)

4 green onions, white part only, thinly sliced

2 lemon-grass stalks, thinly sliced

Pound garlic and chiles in a mortar until crushed to a paste. Place in a small bowl. Stir in lemon juice, fish sauce, soy sauce and Maggi seasoning. Let stand until serving time. Shell shrimp, retaining tail and a small portion of shell attached to shrimp at tail end. Remove sand veins. Preheat broiler. Place shrimp in a single layer in a shallow baking pan. Do not crowd; if necessary, broil in 2 batches. Place shrimp under broiler 3 inches from heat source. Broil 2 minutes or until shrimp are pink throughout; do not overcook. Place shrimp in a large serving bowl. Stir in shallots, green onions and lemon grass. Add lemon-juice mixture; toss to combine. Makes 4 servings.

Noodles with Shrimp, Pork & Vegetables
Pancit Canton (The Philippines)

Filipinos use a dried noodle called pancit canton, *or quick-cooking Japanese* chuka soba. *If you can't get either one, substitute 8 ounces dried spaghetti, cooked in boiling salted water until tender-firm:*

2 oz. small Chinese peapods, about 18

1/4 lb. shrimp, peeled, deveined

1 (8-oz.) pkg. chuka soba noodles

2 tablespoons oil

1/4 lb. lean pork, cut in small thin strips

1 small onion, halved, thinly sliced

3 large garlic cloves, minced

1 small carrot, peeled, thinly sliced crosswise

1/2 small head cabbage, finely sliced (2 to 3 cups)

1 cup chicken broth

1/4 lb. bean sprouts

3 to 4 tablespoons soy sauce

Tops of 2 green onions, sliced crosswise

1 hard-cooked egg, sliced or cut into wedges

Clean peapods and remove stems, pulling off strings at back. Bring 6 cups water to a boil in a large saucepan. Add peapods; boil, uncovered, 1 minute. Remove with a slotted spoon; set aside. Add shrimp; boil 3 minutes. Remove with slotted spoon; set aside. Add noodles; boil 3 minutes, gently pulling apart with a fork. Drain noodles; rinse with cold water. Drain well. Heat oil in a wok or large skillet. Add pork; stir-fry until browned. Add onion, garlic and carrot; stir-fry until onion is tender. Add cabbage and 1/2 cup broth. Cook until cabbage is wilted, about 5 minutes. Add remaining broth and noodles. Add bean sprouts, peapods, shrimp and 3 tablespoons soy sauce. Toss until combined and heated through. Avoid over stirring noodles, which makes them pasty. Taste and add remaining 1 tablespoon soy sauce, if desired. Turn out onto a heated serving platter. Sprinkle with sliced green onion and garnish with hard-cooked egg. Makes 6 servings.

Lychee-Pineapple Dessert

Raum Mit (Thailand)

*Crunchy pieces of ice give welcome relief
from the heat and humidity prevalent in
Thailand.*

**1 (20-oz.) can lychees in heavy
  syrup, chilled**

1/2 cup coconut milk

3 tablespoons sugar

**1/2 cup canned nata de piña
  (pineapple gel) or canned pineapple
  chunks, cut into halves, chilled**

1 cup cracked ice

Drain lychees, reserving syrup.
Combine syrup, coconut milk and
sugar in a small bowl; stir to dissolve
sugar. Cover and refrigerate until
chilled. There will be about 1-1/2
cups sauce. Divide lychees and nata
de piña among 4 large dessert bowls.
Top each serving with some of the
ice. Serve at once. Makes 4 servings.

▲ *Southeast Asians are strikingly
inventive with food, turning
ingredients that most of us have
never heard of into wonderful dishes.
In the Philippines, home economics
students learn to make* nata de
piña, *a delicately flavored pineapple
gel that is served with ice as a
dessert or combined with fruit. The
procedure is long, but, fortunately,
there is commercial nata de piña,
which is exported to Filipino
markets.*

*Other unusual dessert ingredients
include sweetened beans, chewy
palm seeds and a paste made from a
purple yam called* ube. *One of the
prettiest cakes imaginable is the
exotic lavender ube cake. I used to
admire a handsome example in the
bakery of the Manila Hotel, only to
find the same thing in Filipino
bakeries at home.*

Frankly Spicy Stuff

Not all Asians enjoy powerfully spiced food. The Thais serve hot dips on the side and Indonesians provide fiery sambals so that dishes can be seasoned to taste. However, a little chile adds a pleasant zing, and this menu is for those who like that effect. Steamed rice and ice cream provide moments of relief.

MENU

Spicy Lamb Soup

Stir-Fried Steak with Chiles & Bamboo Shoots

Coconut Curried Vegetables

Carrot & Green-Bean Relish

Javanese Hot Sauce, page 18

Steamed Rice

Fruits with Spicy Sweet Sauce

Rum-raisin ice cream, or any favorite flavor

Spicy Lamb Soup

Sop Kambing (Malaysia, Singapore, Indonesia)

Increase the number of dried hot chiles, if you like, or substitute a liberal dash of red (cayenne) pepper.

3/4 lb. lamb bones, with some meat attached

6 cups water

1 medium onion, quartered

3 medium garlic cloves

2 (1/4-inch-thick) gingerroot slices

1 small dried hot chile

1 (3-inch) cinnamon stick

3 whole star anise

6 whole cloves

1-1/2 teaspoons salt

1/4 teaspoon black peppercorns

1 cup coconut milk

1 (6- to 8-oz.) russet potato

1 small carrot

1/2 lb. boneless lean lamb, cut into 1/2-inch chunks

1 medium tomato, cut into thin wedges

2 large green onions, including tops, finely chopped

Place lamb bones in a 3-quart saucepan. Add water; bring to a boil. Skim foam off surface until clear. Add onion, garlic, gingerroot, chile, cinnamon, star anise, cloves, salt and peppercorns. Bring to a boil. Reduce heat and simmer, uncovered, 2 hours, stirring occasionally. Strain broth into another container, reserving bones. Add water, if necessary, to make about 3 cups broth. Rinse saucepan; return broth to saucepan. Stir in coconut milk. Peel potato; cut into 1/2-inch pieces. Cut carrot into 1/2-inch pieces. Cut off any usable meat from bones; add to broth with lamb chunks, potato and carrot. Bring to a boil. Reduce heat, cover and simmer 30 minutes. Add tomato wedges to soup. Simmer 10 minutes. Ladle soup into 4 large bowls; sprinkle with green onions. Makes 4 servings.

Stir-Fried Steak with Chiles & Bamboo Shoots

Pad Prik Nua (Thailand)

Fresh red chiles are becoming more widely available. For vibrant color, use them instead of fresh green chiles.

1 lb. beef flank steak, partially frozen

1/2 cup chicken broth

1 tablespoon fish sauce

1 teaspoon Maggi seasoning

3 tablespoons oil

4 garlic cloves, minced

3 small fresh green chiles, sliced crosswise

1 (8-oz.) can sliced bamboo shoots, drained (1 cup)

1/4 cup lightly packed cilantro leaves

Cut meat with the grain into sections 1-1/2 to 2 inches wide, then cut across the grain into 1/16- to 1/8-inch-thick slices. Combine broth, fish sauce and Maggi seasoning in a small bowl. Heat wok over high heat. Add oil and heat. Add garlic and chiles; stir-fry about 10 seconds. Add meat; cook until most of the red color has gone. Stir in bamboo shoots. Add broth mixture; bring to a boil, stirring. Add cilantro, stir and spoon onto a heated platter. Makes 4 servings.

Coconut Curried Vegetables

Gaeng Keo Wan (Thailand)

Substitute any combination of cooked vegetables in this sauce. Meat may also be added.

1 (14-oz.) can coconut milk
  (1-3/4 cups)
1 tablespoon Green Curry Paste,
  page 15
1 tablespoon fish sauce
1 teaspoon lemon juice
1/2 teaspoon salt
1 (10-oz.) pkg. frozen green peas,
  thawed
1 (15-oz.) can straw mushrooms,
  drained

Combine coconut milk, curry paste, fish sauce, lemon juice and salt in a large saucepan. Bring to a boil. Add peas and mushrooms. Bring to a boil again. Reduce heat, cover and simmer 5 minutes or until vegetables are heated through. Serve in small bowls. Makes 6 servings.

Carrot & Green-Bean Relish

Som Tam Sukothai (Thailand)

Thais might make this relish much hotter, but the following version is spicy enough for most tastes. The carrots should be shredded at an angle into very thin long strands, not finely grated.

6 small dried shrimp

6 green beans

2 tablespoons lemon juice

2 tablespoons water

1 tablespoon fish sauce

1 tablespoon sugar

1 large garlic clove, crushed

1 small fresh red or green chile, sliced crosswise

1/2 lb. carrots, shredded

Soak shrimp in hot water until softened, then pound in a mortar until thoroughly crushed. Cut beans diagonally into thin 1-inch-long slices. Bring 2 cups water to a boil in a small saucepan. Add beans; boil 2 minutes then drain. Rinse with cold water; drain again. Stir lemon juice, water, fish sauce and sugar in a small bowl until sugar dissolves. Add pounded shrimp, garlic and chile. Combine carrots, green beans and dressing in a medium bowl. Cover and refrigerate at least 2 hours to allow flavors to blend. Serve at room temperature. Makes 4 servings.

Fruits with Spicy Sweet Sauce

Naum Pla Van (Thailand)

The unusual dip accompanies a platterful of fruits and cucumber. For a simpler presentation, a single fruit may be used. Look for the coconut in a natural-foods store.

2/3 cup sugar

2 tablespoons light corn syrup

1/4 cup fish sauce

1/4 cup water

4 teaspoons finely ground
   unsweetened dried coconut

1 teaspoon ground dried shrimp

1/4 teaspoon hot red-pepper flakes

Assorted fruits and vegetables
   such as thinly sliced unpeeled tart
   apples, thin jícama wedges,
   thin fresh pineapple wedges, thin
   firm papaya or melon slices and
   thin cucumber slices

Combine sugar, corn syrup, fish sauce and water in a small saucepan. Bring to a full rolling boil. Remove from heat. Stir in coconut, dried shrimp and pepper flakes. Cool to room temperature. If using apples, slice and place in ice water mixed with lemon juice to prevent browning. Use 2 tablespoons lemon juice to 3 cups water for 2 apples. Arrange fruits and vegetables on a large platter. (Without other fruits, 2 apples will make 6 to 8 servings.) Place sauce in a small bowl in center of platter. To eat, dip fruits and vegetables in sauce. Makes 2/3 cup sauce, enough for 6 servings.

Menu from Manila

P hilippine food is the most mildly seasoned in Southeast Asia. Even your most conservative friends would enjoy this meal, and they'll be impressed by the spectacular dessert.

MENU

Green-Mango Shake

Braised Pork with Tomatoes

Steamed rice

Green salad

Mango Jubilee

Green-Mango Shake

Katas ng Berdeng Mangga (The Philippines)

Ripe mangoes can also be used, but the sharper flavor of the unripe green mango adds character to the drink.

1 medium, green (unripe) mango
1 cup cracked ice
3 tablespoons Simple Syrup, page 18

Cut mango pulp away from the seed. Peel flesh. Place mango, ice and syrup in a blender; blend at high speed until puréed. Pour into 1 tall glass or 2 smaller glasses. Makes 1 or 2 servings.

Variation
Combine ingredients for Green-Mango Shake and 2 ounces vodka in a blender. Blend until puréed. Makes 2 servings.

▲ *In Manila supermarkets you can take your choice of ripe yellow or firm green mangoes. Sliced or shredded, the green fruit adds tantalizing, tangy flavor to salads and relishes.*

Most restaurants serve this sweet green mango drink as a refreshing aperitif. I first tasted it at Kamayan, where you eat in traditional style, using your hands. And the seafood is so fresh a live fish flopped its way across the floor to my feet.

Braised Pork with Tomatoes

Apritadang Baboy (The Philippines)

*Spanish and Oriental influences blend
in a hearty stew, ideal for a winter dinner.*

5 tablespoons soy sauce

**1/4 cup palm or unseasoned mild
  vinegar**

3 garlic cloves, crushed

1 bay leaf

1/4 teaspoon black pepper

**2 lbs. boneless, lean pork cut into
  1-1/2-inch chunks**

2 tablespoons oil

1 medium onion, halved, sliced

1 (1-lb.) can peeled whole tomatoes

**2 medium potatoes , peeled, cut
  into eighths**

**1 medium green bell pepper, cut
  into 1-inch squares**

2 tablespoons fine dry bread crumbs

Combine soy sauce, vinegar, garlic, bay leaf and pepper in a glass casserole. Add pork and stir to coat. Cover and marinate in refrigerator 2 hours or longer, turning at least twice to season evenly. Heat oil in a Dutch oven. Add onion; cook until tender but not browned. Add undrained tomatoes. Bring to a boil; cook 3 minutes, mashing tomatoes well. Add pork and marinade. Bring to a boil; reduce heat, cover and simmer 35 minutes. Add potatoes and green pepper; simmer, covered, 20 minutes or until potatoes are tender. Stir in bread crumbs and cook, uncovered, 5 minutes longer. Remove bay leaf. Makes 6 servings.

Mango Jubilee
(The Philippines)

This dessert is so popular in Manila that one constantly sees bursts of flame as the mangoes and their sauce are ignited at tableside.

3 tablespoons butter

1/3 cup sugar

1/2 cup orange juice

1 teaspoon lime juice

1/4 teaspoon grated lime peel

1 cup packed diced fresh mango
(1/2- to 3/4-inch dice)

2 tablespoons triple sec or other
orange-flavored liqueur

1 tablespoon brandy

1 pint vanilla ice cream

Melt butter and sugar in a large skillet or the blazer pan of a chafing dish. Stir in orange juice, lime juice and lime peel. Boil, stirring occasionally, until mixture reduces and becomes syrupy. Add mango; cook 1-1/2 minutes or until mango is heated through. Add triple sec and brandy. Ignite with a long match. Stir until flames subside. Place 2 small scoops ice cream in each dessert bowl. Spoon mango mixture over ice cream. Serve at once. Makes 4 servings.

Satay Barbecue

I f you were to choose one dish as most typical of Southeast Asia, it would probably be satay— grilled meat on a skewer accompanied by peanut sauce. In Singapore, Indonesia or Malaysia, buffets of local foods often include several types of satay, as in the following menu.

MENU

Borneo Dream cocktails

Lamb Satay

Chicken Satay

Vegetable Platter with Peanut Sauce

Shrimp Chips, page 17

Yellow Steamed Rice or Fried Steamed Rice, page 17

Straits Chinese Pineapple Relish

Cantonese Coconut Pudding

Platter of sliced watermelon and pineapple

Borneo Dream
(Brunei)

A long, cool, light drink that will be welcome in hot weather anywhere.

1 oz. (2 tablespoons) vodka
1 oz. (2 tablespoons) crème de cassis
1 oz. (2 tablespoons) triple sec
2 oz. (1/4 cup) orange juice
2 oz. (1/4 cup) pineapple juice
Ice cubes

Combine all ingredients except ice cubes in a cocktail shaker. Shake thoroughly. Strain into a large glass. Add ice cubes. Makes 1 serving.

▲ *The island of Borneo is divided between Malaysia and Indonesia, with a tiny speck left over for Brunei. There, the sultan's palace has different chefs for Western and Asian food, enormous kitchen facilities and specially made carts that rush hot food in moments to an outdoor dining area large enough for 5,000 guests. During Hari Raya, at the end of Ramadan, the sultan holds open house and invites all his subjects to attend. The royal family forms a receiving line and the guests are treated to cool beverages, cookies and other refreshments.*

Lamb Satay

Saté Kambing (Indonesia)

Rich-tasting Indonesian-style soy sauce makes an excellent marinade. If your markets don't carry this sauce, try the recipe on page 16.

2 lbs. trimmed boneless leg of lamb, cut in 3/4-inch cubes

1/4 cup Indonesian-style soy sauce (kecap)

1/2 medium onion, thinly sliced

3 garlic cloves, minced

1/2 teaspoon black pepper

2 tablespoons margarine, softened

Javanese Peanut Sauce:

1/2 medium onion, chopped

2 large garlic cloves

1 small fresh red chile, stemmed, seeded, chopped

1 tablespoon oil

3/4 cup water

1/2 cup creamy peanut butter

2 tablespoons Indonesian-style soy sauce (kecap), page 18

2 teaspoons lime juice

Place lamb in a medium bowl. Add soy sauce, onion, garlic and pepper. Mix well. Cover and refrigerate 2 hours or overnight. Bring lamb to room temperature before grilling. Just before serving, make Javanese Peanut Sauce. Prepare barbecue. Set grill close to coals. Thread lamb onto 20 skewers. Brush meat with margarine. Grill 3 to 5 minutes, or until browned. Turn; brush with margarine; grill 3 to 5 more minutes, or until done as desired. Do not overcook. Serve with peanut sauce. Makes 10 appetizer servings.

Javanese Peanut Sauce:
Chop onion, garlic and chile in blender or food processor fitted with metal blade. Heat oil in a 1-quart saucepan. Add onion mixture; sauté until onion is tender. Return to food processor. Add 1/2 cup water; process mixture until finely ground. Return to saucepan. Add remaining 1/4 cup water, peanut butter, soy sauce and lime juice. Bring to a boil, reduce heat and simmer gently, uncovered, 5 minutes, stirring occasionally. Keep warm; pour into a small bowl just before serving. Makes 1 cup.

Chicken Satay

Satay Gai (Thailand)

Curry powder and crushed gingerroot add zesty flavor to the marinade. Cream and butter are ingredients that distinguish this satay *from other recipes.*

2 whole chicken breasts, boned, skinned

1 teaspoon salt

1/4 teaspoon black pepper

1/2 cup coconut milk

1/2 cup chopped gingerroot (1/4 lb.)

3 tablespoons whipping cream

2 tablespoons butter, melted

1 teaspoon curry powder

1 teaspoon ground coriander

Thai Satay Sauce:

1 cup coconut milk

1 tablespoon creamy peanut butter

2 teaspoons sugar

1 teaspoon Red Curry Paste, page 16

1 teaspoon lemon juice

1/4 teaspoon salt

Cut chicken breasts into strips 1/2 to 3/4 inch wide. Mix with salt and pepper. Combine remaining ingredients in a medium bowl. Stir in chicken. Cover and refrigerate 4 to 6 hours. Bring to room temperature before grilling. Make Thai Satay Sauce. Prepare barbecue. Set grill close to coals. Thread chicken onto 16 skewers. Grill chicken 5 to 8 minutes on each side or until cooked through, turning as needed. Do not overcook. Serve with Thai Satay Sauce. Makes 8 appetizer servings.

Thai Satay Sauce:
Place coconut milk in a small saucepan. Bring to a boil. Stir in remaining ingredients; boil 1 minute, stirring. Keep warm; pour into a small bowl just before serving. Makes 1 cup.

Vegetable Platter with Peanut Sauce
Gado Gado (Indonesia)

For a large party, double or triple recipe and serve Gado Gado *as a salad bar.*

2 small carrots, cut in small chunks

1/4 lb. green beans, cut diagonally
   in 1-1/2-inch slices

1/2 small head cabbage, cut in
   1/2-inch slices

Salt

6 oz. bean sprouts (about 2 cups)

1 medium potato, parboiled, cut in
   1/4-inch slices

2 hard-cooked eggs, cut in wedges

1 small cucumber, peeled, sliced

Shrimp Chips, page 17, if desired

Peanut Sauce:

1 tablespoon oil

1/4 medium onion, finely chopped

1 garlic clove, minced

Dash black pepper

1/2 cup crunchy peanut butter

1/2 cup water

1-1/2 tablespoons Indonesian-style
   soy sauce (kecap), page 18

2 teaspoons lemon juice

1 teaspoon sugar

1/8 teaspoon red (cayenne) pepper,
   if desired

Make Peanut Sauce. Cook carrots, beans and cabbage separately in salted boiling water until tender. Drain, rinse and drain well. Pat dry; set aside. Drop bean sprouts into hot water; let stand 1 minute. Drain, rinse and drain well. Arrange cabbage in center of a large platter. Arrange cooked vegetables, potato, egg wedges and cucumber slices in separate groups around cabbage, making a pleasing pattern. Scatter Shrimp Chips around edge or over top. Serve with Peanut Sauce. Makes 4 to 6 servings.

Peanut Sauce:
Heat oil in a small saucepan over low heat. Add onion, garlic and black pepper; cook slowly until tender and lightly browned. Add peanut butter; stir until melted. Stir in remaining ingredients. Serve warm. Makes 1 cup sauce.

Yellow Steamed Rice

Nasi Kuning (Indonesia)

Indonesians serve this colorful rice on special occasions. The recipe comes from Jakarta.

2 cups coconut milk

1 (1/4-inch-thick) gingerroot slice

1 (2-inch) lemon-grass piece, crushed

1/2 teaspoon ground turmeric

1 teaspoon salt

1 cup long-grain rice, washed, drained

Crisp-Fried Onion Shreds, page 16

1 medium tomato, thinly sliced

1/2 cucumber, thinly sliced

Place coconut milk, gingerroot and lemon grass in a heavy 3-quart saucepan; bring to a boil. Reduce heat; simmer 15 minutes. Strain, discarding gingerroot and lemon grass; return coconut milk to saucepan. Stir in turmeric, salt and rice. Bring to a boil. Reduce heat, cover and simmer until liquid is absorbed, 5 to 10 minutes. Reduce heat to very low; steam without stirring 30 minutes or until rice is tender. Use a heat diffuser if necessary to prevent rice from burning and sticking. Mound rice in center of a large round platter. Sprinkle with fried onions. Alternate tomato and cucumber slices around edge. Makes 4 to 6 servings.

Straits Chinese Pineapple Relish

Acar Nenas (Singapore)

This relish combines pineapple with such unexpected companions as garlic, chile and onion.

1 large cucumber

1/2 medium onion

3 cups small, thin, fresh pineapple wedges

1-1/2 teaspoons salt

1 large garlic clove

1 small fresh red or green chile, sliced crosswise

2 tablespoons white vinegar

2 tablespoons sugar

Peel cucumber. Cut in half lengthwise; scoop out seeds. Cut cucumber crosswise into 1/4-inch-thick slices. Cut onion in half lengthwise, then cut crosswise into thin slices. Combine cucumber, onion and pineapple in a medium bowl. Stir in salt. Let stand 1 hour. Take small handfuls of mixture at a time; squeeze out as much liquid as possible. Place in another bowl. Let stand 30 minutes. Drain off any liquid that has accumulated. Pound garlic with chile in a mortar to form a paste. Stir garlic paste, vinegar and sugar in a small cup until sugar dissolves. Stir dressing into pineapple mixture. Cover and marinate in refrigerator at least 2 hours before serving. Makes about 2 cups or 6 to 8 small servings.

Cantonese Coconut Pudding

Ya Tze Bo Din (Malaysia)

*Double or triple the recipe for a party.
Serve the pudding plain or decorate with
a fan of strawberry slices or mandarin-
orange segments.*

1/3 cup sugar
3 tablespoons cornstarch
2 cups coconut milk

Combine sugar and cornstarch in
a medium saucepan. Gradually stir
in coconut milk. Cook, stirring, over
medium heat until mixture thickens
and comes to a boil. Boil 1 minute.
Spoon mixture into 4 custard cups or
small ramekins. Serve warm or
chilled. Makes 4 servings.

▲ *Ibu Ida Ayu Agung Mas, who gave
me a cooking lesson at her village
home in Bali, picked the coconuts we
needed from her yard. Sweet and
fresh, they gave subtle flavor to the
satay we were making and a green-
bean salad. The coconuts available in
western countries tend to be old and
less desirable for cooking. That's why
it's often better to use canned, frozen
or dehydrated coconut milk than to
make your own.*

Chinese New Year Celebration

The large Chinese population of cities like Singapore, where several of these recipes were gathered, guarantees a lively welcome to the New Year.

MENU

Gong Hee Fat Choy cocktail

Crab & Asparagus Soup

Beef with Fried Walnuts

Sweet & Sour Pickled Fish

Stir-Fried Cabbage & Eggs

Steamed rice

Water-Chestnut Pudding

Almond Cookies

Chinese New Year Cocktail
Gong Hee Fat Choy (Singapore)

The traditional Chinese New Year salutation serves as the title of this drink.

1 oz. (2 tablespoons) gin
3/4 oz. (1-1/2 tablespoons) Napoleon
  Mandarine Liqueur
1 oz. (2 tablespoons) orange juice
3/4 oz. (1-1/2 tablespoons) lime juice
1/2 teaspoon Simple Syrup,
  page 18
1/4 teaspoon grenadine
3 or 4 ice cubes

Combine all ingredients in a cocktail shaker. Shake thoroughly. Strain into a stemmed glass. Makes 1 serving.

▲ *I've never been to Singapore during Chinese New Year, but there's excitement enough at Christmas when Orchard Road, lined with shopping centers and hotels, turns into a fantastic corridor of illuminated buildings. At the Hilton, in upper Orchard Road, I celebrated with this drink. Sweet with fresh juices, it's delightful in hot weather, which Singapore experiences all year.*

Crab & Asparagus Soup

Xup Mang Cua (Vietnam)

The base of this soup is Oriental-style chicken broth seasoned with gingerroot and green onions. Try using the broth in other soups, too.

1 (6-oz.) can crabmeat

18 spears canned peeled small white asparagus

2 eggs

6 cilantro sprigs

Oriental Chicken Broth:

Carcass portion of 4 chicken-breast halves or 1 chicken carcass or 3 chicken backs

2 green onions, including part of the tops, cut into 1-inch lengths

2 (1/4-inch-thick) gingerroot slices

6-1/2 cups water

1 tablespoon chicken-bouillon granules

3/4 teaspoon salt

Prepare Oriental Chicken Broth. Place in a 3-quart saucepan. Drain crabmeat. Place in a sieve; rinse. Add to broth. Cut asparagus spears into thirds; there will be about 1 cup. Add asparagus to broth. Simmer gently, uncovered, 10 minutes. Beat eggs in a small bowl. Slowly pour eggs into soup, stirring constantly to form egg threads. Spoon into soup bowls. Top each serving with a cilantro sprig. Makes 6 servings.

Oriental Chicken Broth:
Combine all ingredients in a 3-quart saucepan. Bring to a rolling boil. Skim surface. Reduce heat, cover and simmer 1 hour. Strain broth. If desired, make broth ahead, cover and refrigerate until chilled. Remove any fat from surface before using. Makes about 6 cups.

Beef with Fried Walnuts

Her Tao Niu Rou (Singapore)

Crunchy deep-fried walnuts make an interesting contrast to the tender beef in this Cantonese dish.

1 lb. beef flank steak or any tender steak, partially frozen

1/3 cup chicken broth

1 teaspoon soy sauce

1 teaspoon oyster sauce

1/2 teaspoon sesame oil

1/2 teaspoon salt

Dash white pepper

1 teaspoon cornstarch

2 cups oil

1 cup walnut halves

3 green onions, white part only, cut into 1-inch lengths

1 (2-inch) piece carrot, thinly sliced

1-1/2 tablespoons thinly sliced gingerroot

Cut steak with the grain into sections 1-1/2 to 2 inches wide, then cut across the grain into slices 1/16 to 1/8 inch thick. Combine chicken broth, soy sauce, oyster sauce, sesame oil, salt, pepper and cornstarch in a small bowl; set aside. Heat a wok over medium-high heat. Add 1 cup of the oil; heat to 360F (180C) or until a 1-inch bread cube turns golden brown in 60 seconds. Add walnuts; fry until nuts start to brown, about 3 minutes. Remove with a slotted spoon; drain on paper towels. Add remaining 1 cup oil to wok; heat to 360F (180C). Add beef; fry, stirring, until browned, about 1 minute. Using a slotted spoon, transfer beef to a bowl or plate. Drain off oil from wok, leaving about 1 tablespoon. Add onions, carrot and gingerroot; stir-fry 30 seconds. Return beef and walnuts to wok; stir-fry 1 minute. Stir cornstarch mixture. Add to wok; cook, stirring, until mixture thickens and coats meat and vegetables. Makes 4 servings.

Sweet & Sour Pickled Fish

Acar Ikan (Brunei)

A delightful contrast of flavors.

1 (1-1/2-lb.) cleaned whole red snapper, excluding head and tail, or thick-cut fish steaks

2 teaspoons salt

1 teaspoon ground turmeric

2 small cucumbers, peeled

2/3 cup white vinegar

1/4 cup sugar

1/2 teaspoon ground turmeric

1/4 teaspoon salt

2 cups oil

2 small onions, halved lengthwise, thinly sliced

2 (1/2-inch-thick) gingerroot slices, cut into thin strips 1/2 inch wide

1 small fresh red chile, sliced lengthwise

1 green chile, sliced lengthwise

2 large garlic cloves, chopped

Cut fish into small individual portions. Sprinkle fish with 2 teaspoons salt and 1 teaspoon turmeric. Let stand at room temperature 1 hour. Cut cucumbers in half lengthwise; scoop out seeds. Cut lengthwise into thin slices; set aside. Mix vinegar, sugar, remaining 1/2 teaspoon turmeric and salt in a small bowl until sugar dissolves; set aside. Heat oil in a wok to 360F (180C). Add fish pieces, a few at a time; fry until they turn opaque when tested with a fork and are lightly browned, 4 to 8 minutes depending upon thickness of fish. Drain on paper towels; keep warm. Drain off oil, reserving 2 tablespoons. Clean wok. Reheat reserved oil in wok. Add cucumbers, onions, gingerroot, chiles and garlic; stir-fry 1 minute. Add vinegar mixture. Boil, uncovered, 5 minutes. Place fish portions on a heated large platter. Top with vegetable mixture, including any liquid in wok. Makes 4 servings.

Stir-Fried Cabbage & Eggs

Kobis Dan Telur (Malaysia)

This Chinese-style dish was demonstrated during a cooking class at the Kuala Lumpur YWCA.

1 head green cabbage, (1-1/2 lbs.), quartered, cored

4 eggs

1-1/2 tablespoons oil

1-1/2 teaspoons butter

2 garlic cloves, minced

1/4 lb. medium shrimp, shelled, deveined, minced or finely ground

1/4 lb. lean pork, minced or finely ground

1 (6-oz.) red onion, halved lengthwise, thinly sliced

1 teaspoon salt

1/4 teaspoon black pepper

Cut cabbage crosswise into thin slices; set aside. Break eggs into a small bowl; do not beat. Set aside. Heat oil and butter in a wok or large non-stick skillet. Add garlic; cook until garlic starts to brown. Add shrimp and pork; cook, stirring, until mixture is lightly browned. Add onion and cabbage; stir until cabbage starts to wilt. Add eggs, salt and pepper. Stir to break up eggs and combine with cabbage. Cook until eggs are set and mixture is dry. Makes 6 large servings.

Water-Chestnut Pudding

Ping Hua Ma Ti Lu (Singapore)

A pudding in name only, this dessert is more accurately described as a lightly thickened sweet soup.

2-2/3 cups water

1/2 cup sugar

3/4 cup canned water chestnuts (about 24), cut in very small dice

2 tablespoons cornstarch

2 tablespoons cold water

1 egg, beaten

Combine 2-2/3 cups water and sugar in a 1-quart saucepan. Bring to a boil, stirring until sugar has dissolved. Add water chestnuts; bring to a boil again. Blend cornstarch and 2 tablespoons cold water in a small bowl. Stir into boiling mixture; cook until slightly thickened, stirring frequently. Remove from heat. Add egg; stir to form shreds. Serve in soup bowls. Makes 4 servings.

▲ *A typical Cantonese dessert that's very nice following a spicy meal. I like to serve it in small Chinese rice bowls.*

Steak & French Fries, Vietnamese Style

A restaurant in Ho Chi Minh City pairs this hot beef salad with French fries. When entertaining, round out the menu with a brightly seasoned chicken dish.

MENU

French onion soup or shrimp cocktail

Hot Beef Salad

Lemon-Grass Chicken

French fries

Chocolate mousse

Hot Beef Salad

Bo Luc Lac (Vietnam)

Stir-fried beef combines with tomato and lettuce for this main-dish salad. Sizzling individual metal platters with wood bases are attractive for the presentation.

1 (1-lb.) flank steak, partially frozen
2 tablespoons soy sauce
1 tablespoon oil
1/2 teaspoon sugar
3 garlic cloves, minced
1 medium onion, cut in eighths
2 small dried hot chiles
2 tablespoons soy sauce
2 tablespoons beef broth
5 tablespoons oil
1/2 teaspoon sugar
12 red-leaf-lettuce leaves
2 medium tomatoes, each cut into
    6 slices
16 cilantro sprigs

Cut meat with the grain in 2 or 3 strips; cut strips diagonally across the grain into 1/8-inch-thick slices. Place in a medium bowl. Add 2 tablespoons soy sauce, 1 tablespoon oil, 1/2 teaspoon sugar and garlic. Mix well. Cover and refrigerate 2 hours. Mix again and bring to room temperature before cooking. Separate onion layers; set aside. Soak chiles in warm water about 30 minutes or until softened. Discard seeds and stems; mince chiles. Combine chiles, remaining 2 tablespoons soy sauce and beef broth in a small bowl. Heat a wok; add 4 tablespoons oil. Add onion; stir-fry 1 minute. Remove onion with a slotted spoon, draining oil back into wok; place onion in a small bowl. Stir-fry steak 3 minutes. Remove steak and any liquid in wok; add to onion. Heat remaining 1 table-spoon oil in wok. Add remaining 1/2 teaspoon sugar. When sugar melts, stir in chile mixture. Return steak and onion to wok, stir-fry 1 minute. Remove from heat. Arrange 3 lettuce leaves on each plate. Place 1/4 of beef in center of each serving. Garnish with tomato slices and cilantro sprigs. Makes 4 servings.

Lemon-Grass Chicken

Ga Xao Sa Ot (Vietnam)

Chicken breast meat is regarded as a delicacy by some, but the juicier and less expensive dark meat is preferred for this dish.

6 chicken thighs, boned, skinned (about 1-1/4 lbs. trimmed meat)

2 lemon-grass stalks, minced

1/4 cup soy sauce

1/4 teaspoon salt

2 tablespoons chicken broth

1 teaspoon sugar

1 teaspoon minced small fresh red or green chile or 1/4 teaspoon hot-pepper flakes

1/2 teaspoon cornstarch

2 teaspoons water

1/2 medium onion, cut in fourths

1/4 cup oil

1 teaspoon minced onion

1 teaspoon minced gingerroot

1 teaspoon minced garlic

Cut chicken into 1-inch pieces. Place in a medium bowl. Stir in lemon grass, 2 tablespoons of the soy sauce and salt; mix well. Cover and refrigerate 2 hours or longer. Bring to room temperature before cooking. Combine chicken broth, remaining 2 tablespoons soy sauce, sugar and chile in a small bowl; set aside. Blend cornstarch with water; set aside. Separate onion into layers. Heat a wok. Add oil and heat. Add minced onion, gingerroot and garlic; stir-fry 15 seconds. Do not burn. Increase heat. Add chicken; stir-fry 2 minutes. Add onion layers; stir-fry 1 minute. Add chicken-broth mixture; cook, stirring, 1 minute. Stir cornstarch mixture. Add to chicken mixture; cook until sauce is thickened, about 30 seconds. Spoon onto a heated platter; serve at once. Makes 4 servings.

Two-Way Thai Dinner

T hai restaurants often prepare their dishes with a choice of chicken, meat or seafood. You could, for example, order either chicken or shrimp cooked with mint and green chiles. When substituting one for the other in these recipes, remember that chicken, which should be cut into strips or bite-size pieces, will take slightly longer to cook and that shrimp is done in 4 to 5 minutes. Overcooking toughens it.

MENU

Shrimp with Mint & Chiles or Chicken with Mint & Green Peppers

Mixed Salad & Won-Ton Crisps

Steamed rice or Baked Yellow Steamed Rice, page 39

Corn & Coconut Porridge

Shrimp with Mint & Chiles

Goong Bai Kaprow (Thailand)

Here's a recipe to rely on when you need a company dish that takes almost no time to cook.

3 small fresh green chiles, sliced

2 large garlic cloves

2/3 cup chicken broth

1 teaspoon sugar

1/2 teaspoon salt

2 tablespoons oil

1 lb. medium shrimp, shelled, deveined

1/2 cup lightly packed mint leaves

Pound chiles and garlic in a mortar until well crushed. Spoon into a small cup; set aside. Combine chicken broth, sugar and salt in a small bowl; set aside. Heat a wok over high heat. Add oil and heat. Stir in chile mixture. Immediately add broth mixture; bring to a boil. Add shrimp; cook, stirring, about 2 minutes or just until shrimp turn pink. Stir in mint leaves; cook until wilted, about 30 seconds. Spoon onto a heated platter. Makes 4 servings.

Chicken with Mint & Green Peppers

Gai Pad Kaprow (Thailand)

Notice that Thais do not follow the Chinese practice of thickening their sauces with cornstarch.

1-1/2 whole chicken breasts, boned, skinned

1 large garlic clove

1 or 2 small fresh green chiles, stemmed, seeded, chopped

2 medium, green bell peppers

1/2 cup chicken broth

1 tablespoon fish sauce

2 teaspoons oyster sauce

2 teaspoons sugar

3 tablespoons oil

1/2 cup lightly packed mint leaves

Cut chicken into 3/4- to 1-inch chunks; set aside. Pound garlic and chile to a paste in a mortar; set aside. Cut bell peppers lengthwise into 1/2-inch-wide strips, removing seeds and any white membrane. Cut strips in half crosswise; set aside. Combine chicken broth, fish sauce, oyster sauce and sugar in a small bowl. Heat a wok over high heat. Add oil and heat. Add chile paste; stir-fry 10 seconds. Add chicken; stir-fry 3 to 4 minutes or until chicken is no longer pink. Add broth mixture; bring to a boil. Boil, stirring, 3 to 4 minutes. Add green peppers and mint. Cook, stirring, 1 minute, or until peppers are heated through. Do not overcook or peppers lose their bright color. Spoon onto a heated platter; serve. Makes 4 small servings.

Mixed Salad & Won-Ton Crisps

Yam Yai (Thailand)

A beautiful, colorful salad.

8 square won-ton wrappers
Oil for deep-frying
8 romaine-lettuce leaves
2 pickling cucumbers, cut
  diagonally in thin slices
2 medium tomatoes, halved, sliced
2 hard-cooked eggs, each cut into
  6 wedges
1 cup finely shredded red cabbage
1/2 cup coarsely shredded carrot

Peanut Dressing:
2/3 cup creamy peanut butter
1 cup coconut milk
4 teaspoons sugar
1/4 to 1/2 teaspoon salt
2 tablespoons lime juice
1/4 teaspoon hot-pepper sauce

Make Peanut Dressing. Separate won-ton wrappers, then restack and cut into 3/4-inch squares. Heat 1/2 inch oil in a small skillet. Add won-tons a few at a time; fry until lightly browned. Drain on paper towels; set aside. Cut lettuce crosswise into 1/2-inch slices. Arrange in mounds in centers of salad plates. Arrange cucumber slices and tomatoes around lettuce. Place 3 egg wedges around lettuce on each plate. Top lettuce with cabbage, then carrot shreds. Spoon 1/4 cup Peanut Dressing over each salad. Sprinkle with fried won tons. Pass remaining dressing. Makes 4 servings.

Peanut Dressing:
Combine peanut butter, coconut milk, sugar and salt to taste in a small saucepan. Stir over low heat just until blended. Remove from heat; stir in lime juice and hot-pepper sauce. Serve at room temperature. Makes 1-1/2 cups.

Corn & Coconut Porridge

Bubur Jagung (Malaysia)

Although this recipe comes from Malaysia, it fits very well into a Thai meal.

1 (17-oz.) can cream-style corn
1-1/2 cups coconut milk
1/4 cup packed dark-brown sugar
1 tablespoon granulated sugar

Combine ingredients in a 1-1/2-quart saucepan. Bring to a boil, stirring to dissolve sugars. Remove from heat. Serve warm or chilled. Spoon into bowls. Makes 6 servings.

▲ *Whoever heard of corn for dessert? The answer is, almost everyone in Southeast Asia. I've had corn sauce over ice cream in Bangkok, corn ice cream in Penang, corn in a pudding in the Philippines and corn combined with beans, palm seeds, jackfruit and grass jelly in es kacang, an ice-topped food stall treat in Singapore.*

Elegant But Easy Dinner Party

First impressions are important, so start with one of the most popular Thai soups. Arrange the beef and zucchini on separate platters and the rice in a bowl so guests can serve themselves. If you prefer chicken, Marion's dish is easy to prepare ahead and has a wonderful flavor.

MENU

Chicken-Coconut Soup

Stir-Fried Beef & Vegetables or

Marion's Javanese Roast Chicken

Steamed rice

Braised zucchini strips

Ginger Ice Cream

Chicken-Coconut Soup

Tom Kha Gai (Thailand)

Refined, but with a dash of spice, this soup makes an elegant first course. The lime leaves add subtle citrus flavor but can be omitted.

1 large chicken-breast half

3 cups water

1 teaspoon salt

1 (14-oz.) can coconut milk (1-3/4 cups)

1/2 cup drained canned straw mushrooms or button mushrooms

1 lemon-grass stalk, sliced diagonally into 1-inch pieces

4 kaffir lime leaves, cut into large pieces

1 or 2 small fresh red chiles, stemmed, quartered lengthwise, seeded

2 tablespoons fish sauce or additional salt to taste

1 teaspoon ground dried galingal

2 tablespoons lime juice

2 tablespoons fresh basil, cilantro or mint leaves

Place chicken breast, water and salt in a large saucepan. Bring to a boil, cover and simmer 30 minutes. Drain chicken; cool slightly. Remove skin and bones; shred meat. Return chicken meat and 2 cups broth to saucepan. Save remaining broth for another use. Add remaining ingredients except lime juice and herb leaves. Bring to a boil. Reduce heat, cover and simmer 30 minutes. Stir in lime juice. Ladle into individual bowls; garnish with a few basil, cilantro or mint leaves. Additional lime leaves can also be used for garnish, if desired. Makes 4 servings.

Stir-Fried Beef & Vegetables

Bo Xao (Vietnam)

Chinese influence is apparent in the cooking technique and ingredients of this dish. The exception is port wine, a European touch.

1 lb. beef flank steak, partially frozen

1 teaspoon cornstarch

2 tablespoons soy sauce

1 tablespoon port wine

2 garlic cloves, crushed, minced

1 tablespoon finely chopped onion

1/2 teaspoon sugar

1/8 teaspoon black pepper

6 small dried Oriental black mushrooms

1 medium green or red bell pepper

1/2 medium onion, halved lengthwise

1/4 cup chicken broth

1 teaspoon soy sauce

1/2 teaspoon cornstarch

4 tablespoons oil

1/4 teaspoon salt

Cut meat with the grain into sections 2 inches wide, cut strips diagonally across the grain into slices 1/8 inch thick. Place in a medium bowl; mix in 1 teaspoon cornstarch, then add 2 tablespoons soy sauce, port wine, garlic, chopped onion, sugar and black pepper and stir well. Cover and refrigerate 1 to 2 hours. Bring to room temperature before cooking. Meanwhile, soak mushrooms in water until softened. Remove and discard stems; cut into thin slices. Cut bell pepper into 1 x 1/3-inch strips. Cut onion halves into wedges 1/3 inch thick at widest point; separate layers. Mix chicken broth, remaining 1 teaspoon soy sauce and 1/2 teaspoon cornstarch in a small bowl; set aside. Heat a wok. Add 2 tablespoons oil. Stir-fry mushrooms, bell pepper and onion 1 minute. Add salt. Transfer from wok to a dish. Heat remaining 2 tablespoons oil in wok. Add meat; stir-fry 2 minutes or until browned. Return vegetables to wok; stir-fry 1 minute. Stir cornstarch mixture. Add to wok; cook, stirring, until sauce thickens, about 45 seconds. Add salt. Spoon onto a heated platter. Makes 4 servings.

Marion's Javanese Roast Chicken
(Indonesia)

*There's no last-minute work, which
makes this chicken ideal party fare. It's
good cold too.*

**1 (3-1/2- to 3-3/4-lb.) chicken, halved
or quartered**
**1/4 cup Indonesian-style soy sauce
(kecap), page 18**
2 large garlic cloves, minced
**1-1/2 to 2 inches fresh gingerroot,
peeled, grated**
2 tablespoons white wine
1 tablespoon oil

Wash chicken pieces and pat dry
with paper towels. Place chicken in a
single layer in a shallow baking dish.
Combine soy sauce, garlic,
gingerroot, wine and oil. Pour over
chicken and turn to coat well. Cover
and refrigerate 4 to 5 hours. Turn at
least twice. Bring to room
temperature before cooking. Preheat
oven to 350F (175C). Spray a
13 x 9-inch baking pan with
non-stick spray. Place chicken,
skin-side up, in pan. Pour remaining
marinade over and bake 1 hour.
Baste during final 30 minutes. Cut
chicken apart before serving. Makes
4 servings.

Ginger Ice Cream
Ice Krem Khing (Thailand)

Thai restaurants in the United States often serve ginger-flavored ice cream. This is an easy way to make it.

1 pint vanilla ice cream

1/3 cup finely chopped, preserved ginger packed in syrup

1 tablespoon syrup from preserved ginger

1 teaspoon ground ginger

Soften ice cream. Stir in chopped ginger, ginger syrup and ground ginger. Refreeze. Makes 4 servings.

Dinner at the Sultan's Palace

The imposing palace of the Sultan of Brunei yielded these recipes for sumptuous Malay-style chicken curry and rice. As Muslims, the sultan and his entourage consumed only non-alcoholic drinks such as the refreshing Kampong Air, named for a village built on stilts over the water.

MENU

Kampong Air

Brunei-Style Chicken Curry

Celebration Rice

Steamed asparagus or other green vegetable

Coconut Crêpes

Soft drinks, tea, coffee

Kampong Air
(Brunei)

On a summer afternoon, make a pitcherful of this drink, then stir in the soda just before serving.

3 oz. (6 tablespoons) canned mango nectar

1/2 oz. (1 tablespoon) lemon-lime soda or lemonade

1/2 oz. (1 tablespoon) grenadine

1/2 oz. (1 tablespoon) lime juice

Crushed ice

3 oz. (6 tablespoons) lemon-lime soda

Ice cubes

Combine all ingredients except 3 ounces soda and ice cubes in a cocktail shaker. Shake well. Strain into a tall glass. Add remaining soda; stir. Add ice cubes. Makes 1 serving.

▲ Kampong *is the Malay word for village, and* air *means water. Although the name may be exotic, this drink will suit a hot summer day anywhere.*

Brunei-Style Chicken Curry

Gulai Ayam (Brunei)

*Lots of rich gravy makes this mildly
seasoned dish ideal to serve with rice.*

1 (3-1/2-lb.) chicken

3 tablespoons oil

1 medium onion, finely chopped

4 large garlic cloves, finely chopped

1 (1-inch-thick) gingerroot piece,
   minced

1 (1-inch) cinnamon stick

3 green cardamom pods

2 whole cloves

1 whole star anise

3 tablespoons curry powder

1 to 1-1/2 lbs. russet potatoes,
   peeled, cut into large chunks

4 cups coconut milk

2 teaspoons salt

3 medium tomatoes, each cut into
   8 wedges

Cut up chicken. Discard wing
tips. Separate thighs from drumsticks.
Cut breast in half lengthwise and
crosswise, discarding bone if
desired. Remove fat and excess skin.
Heat oil in a Dutch oven. Add onion,
garlic, gingerroot, cinnamon stick,
cardamom pods, cloves and star
anise; sauté 3 minutes. Stir in curry
powder and cook 2 minutes longer.
Add chicken and potatoes; stir to
mix with spices. Add coconut milk
and salt; bring to a boil. Reduce heat,
cover loosely and simmer 45
minutes. Add tomato wedges; cook,
uncovered, 15 minutes longer. Makes
6 servings.

▲ Gulai *is the name used in Brunei
for curry. The Executive Chef for
Malay food, in the Sultan's palace,
provided me with this recipe.*

Celebration Rice

Nasi Biryani (Brunei)

Golden rice accented with almonds and cashews is indeed regal banquet fare.

2 tablespoons vegetable oil

3 tablespoons finely sliced shallots

1/4 cup minced shallots

1 teaspoon minced gingerroot

1 garlic clove, minced

1-1/2 teaspoons salt

1/2 teaspoon ground turmeric

2-1/4 cups water

1-1/4 cups long-grain rice, washed, drained

1/4 cup plain yogurt

1/2 small tomato, sliced

1 tablespoon chopped cilantro

1 tablespoon chopped blanched almonds

1 tablespoon chopped raw cashews

1/2 small fresh red chile, in 1 piece, if desired

Heat oil in a small skillet. Add sliced shallots; fry until golden brown. Drain on paper towel; set aside. Strain oil. There should be about 1 tablespoon. Transfer oil to a large saucepan and heat. Add minced shallots, gingerroot and garlic; sauté 2 minutes. Stir in salt and turmeric. Add water; bring to a boil. Add rice and yogurt, stirring until yogurt is blended. Add tomato, cilantro, nuts and chile, if desired. Cover and simmer over low heat about 40 minutes, or until water is absorbed and rice is tender. Add heat diffuser if necessary to keep rice from overcooking and sticking to pan. Spoon into heated serving dish; garnish with reserved fried shallots. Makes 6 servings.

Coconut Crêpes

Kueh Gulong (Brunei, Indonesia, Malaysia, Singapore)

These bright-green, coconut-filled crêpes can be served with either coconut or chocolate sauce.

2 eggs
3/4 cup coconut milk or water
1/2 cup all-purpose flour
Dash salt
1/8 teaspoon green food color
Vegetable shortening
Coconut Sauce, page 104
Toasted coconut, if desired

Coconut Filling:
1/2 cup packed dark-brown sugar
1/3 cup water
1-1/2 cups flaked coconut

Beat eggs in a medium bowl. Beat in coconut milk, flour, salt and food color. Batter should be bright green. Cover and let stand at room temperature 1 hour. Heat a 6-inch skillet over medium-high heat. Grease lightly with shortening. Pour scant 1/4 cup batter into skillet, swirl quickly to coat bottom. Cook until crêpe appears dry, about 30 seconds. Turn and cook 20 to 25 seconds on other side. Remove crêpe; stack on a plate. Cover and cool. Prepare Coconut Filling. When filling crêpes, keep the side cooked last on the outside. Place 1 rounded tablespoon filling in a strip across crêpe 1/3 of the way from 1 edge. Roll up tightly. Fill remaining crêpes. Serve at room temperature topped with Coconut Sauce. Sprinkle with toasted coconut, if desired. Makes eight crêpes, 4 servings.

Coconut Filling:
Combine brown sugar and water in a small saucepan. Bring to a boil. Add coconut. Cook, stirring, until blended and liquid has almost disappeared. Cool thoroughly, stirring occasionally.

Open-Air Dinner in Bali

S atri's Warung is a tiny restaurant that opens onto a lane in Ubud, a Balinese center of art and music. The word *warung* means *a modest eating place*, but Satri's food is far from humble. Grilled chicken is one of her specialties. She also makes a superior version of the unusual Indonesian dessert, black rice pudding.

MENU

Avocado Cooler

Grilled Chicken Breast with Balinese Sauce

Vegetables in Coconut Milk

Steamed rice

Black Rice Pudding
or
Assorted fresh fruits:
pineapple, mango, watermelon, banana

Avocado Cooler

Es Advokat (Indonesia)

You may be surprised to learn that avocados are used for drinks and desserts in Indonesia.

1 small, very ripe avocado
1/3 cup sweetened condensed milk
2 teaspoons sugar or to taste
2 cups cracked ice
Lemon slice, if desired, for garnish

Combine ingredients in a blender; blend until avocado is pureed and ice is reduced to fine granules. Garnish with lemon slice, if desired. Makes 2 servings.

▲ *This recipe comes from Bali. However, I've enjoyed the same drink in Java, where it was topped with chocolate syrup. Sometimes it's flavored with coffee extract.*

Grilled Chicken Breast with Balinese Sauce

Ayam Panggang Bali (Indonesia)

Indonesian chickens are small and tasty, so you should choose small chicken breasts for this dish.

4 chicken-breast halves

2 large or 3 medium garlic cloves

1/2 teaspoon salt

1/8 teaspoon white pepper

Balinese Sauce:

1-1/2 tablespoons butter

1/4 lb. shallots, peeled, sliced, or 3/4 cup thinly sliced onions

1 large garlic clove, minced

1/2 lb. tomatoes, coarsely chopped

About 1/2 small fresh red chile, sliced

1 teaspoon soy sauce

1/4 teaspoon salt

Dash white pepper

1/2 teaspoon lime juice

Wash chicken well and pat dry. Remove and discard any excess skin and fat. Crush garlic cloves in a mortar. Add salt and pound to a paste. Spread garlic mixture evenly over skin side of chicken. Sprinkle with pepper. Cover and refrigerate at least 2 hours. Prepare Balinese Sauce. Preheat broiler. Place chicken, skin-side up, on a broiler rack not too close to heat. Broil 12 minutes. Turn chicken over and broil 5 minutes longer, or until meat is cooked through. Top each breast with 1/4 of the Balinese Sauce. Makes 4 servings.

Balinese Sauce:
Heat butter in a skillet. Add shallots or onion and garlic; cook until tender. Add tomatoes and chile as desired. Cook until tomatoes are tender. Stir in soy sauce, salt and pepper. Add lime juice just before serving.

Vegetables in Coconut Milk

Sayur Lodeh (Indonesia)

Spoon the sayur *onto steamed rice to capture the fragrant sauce.*

Shells from 1/2 lb. medium shrimp
2 cups water
1-1/2 cups coconut milk
1 lemon-grass stalk, pounded
4 (1/8-inch-thick) slices thawed
  frozen galingal root or 1 teaspoon
  ground dried galingal
2 teaspoons salt
1/8 teaspoon ground turmeric
1/2 lb. green cabbage
1 medium carrot
8 green beans
1/2 medium chayote, peeled, cut
  into 1-inch chunks (1 cup chunks)
1/2 cup (1/4-inch-thick slices)
  canned young corn
1/2 cup cooked tiny shrimp
Steamed rice

Wash shrimp shells. Package and freeze shrimp for another use. Place shells and water in a 1-quart saucepan. Bring to a boil. Reduce heat, cover and simmer 30 minutes. Strain broth. Measure and add water to make 2 cups. Place shrimp broth, coconut milk, lemon grass, galingal, salt and turmeric in a 3-quart saucepan. Cut cabbage half in half again; remove core. Cut crosswise into 1-inch slices. Quarter carrot lengthwise. Cut crosswise into 1-inch pieces. Cut green beans diagonally into 1-inch pieces. Add cabbage, carrot, green beans, chayote and corn to saucepan. Bring to a boil. Reduce heat, cover and simmer 20 to 30 minutes or until all vegetables are tender. Add cooked tiny shrimp; cook 1 minute to heat. Remove lemon grass. Spoon into a heated serving bowl. Serve with steamed rice. Makes 6 servings.

Black Rice Pudding

Bubur Ketan Hitam (Indonesia)

Black glutinous rice, pandan leaves and pandan flavoring can be found in Thai markets and Asian stores that carry Southeast Asian products. If you can't get them, pour the sauce into a bowl, sweeten to taste and add sliced bananas or mangoes.

1 cup black glutinous rice, washed, drained

4 cups water

1 fresh-frozen pandan leaf or several pieces dried pandan leaf or few drops pandan flavoring

1 cup dark-brown or palm sugar

Coconut Sauce:
1 (14-oz.) can coconut milk
1/2 teaspoon vanilla extract
1/4 teaspoon salt

Combine rice, water and pandan leaf or flavoring in a large saucepan. Cover and bring to a boil. Reduce heat and simmer gently 30 minutes. Add sugar; simmer gently 30 minutes longer, or until rice is tender and has consistency of a moderately thick porridge. If too thick, add water as needed. Keep warm. Just before serving, prepare Coconut Sauce. Serve porridge hot, warm, or at room temperature. Spoon into individual bowls and top with several spoonfuls of Coconut Sauce. Makes 4 to 6 servings.

Coconut Sauce:
Shake can of coconut milk well. Open and pour into small bowl. If very thick, dilute with a little water. Stir in vanilla and salt.

Curry Tiffin Lunch in Singapore

The old Raffles Hotel in Singapore was a gathering spot for British colonials who sipped tea or gin slings, depending upon the hour. That era is long gone and the hotel is newly refurbished, but the memories linger on. This is the sort of curry lunch the colonials used to enjoy.

MENU

Singapore Gin Sling

Raffles' Anglo-Indian Chicken Curry

Eggplant Curry

Curry Condiments: Flaked coconut, chopped roasted peanuts or almonds, diced red onion or shallots, chopped hard-cooked egg, diced pineapple, raisins, mango chutney

Sliced cucumbers and tomatoes

Steamed rice

Tapioca Pudding with Two Sauces

Singapore Gin Sling
(Singapore)

This famous drink originated at the Raffles Hotel and has made its way around the world.

2 oz. (1/4 cup) gin
1 oz. (2 tablespoons) cherry brandy
1/3 oz. (2 teaspoons) orange juice
1/3 oz. (2 teaspoons) lime juice
1/3 oz. (2 teaspoons) pineapple juice
1 teaspoon Benedictine liqueur
1 teaspoon triple sec
1/2 teaspoon grenadine
4 drops aromatic bitters
Ice cubes
1-1/2 oz. (3 tablespoons) club soda
Pineapple wedge and maraschino cherry for garnish

Combine gin, cherry brandy, orange, lime and pineapple juices, Benedictine, triple sec, grenadine and bitters in a cocktail shaker. Add 3 or 4 ice cubes, shake well and strain into a large glass. Add soda and additional ice. Garnish with pineapple wedge and cherry strung on a pick. Makes 1 serving.

Raffles' Anglo-Indian Chicken Curry

Kari Ayam (Singapore)

*This is a two-in-one recipe. Serve with
rice and curry condiments.*

1 (3-1/2- to 4-lb.) chicken, cut-up

2-1/2 cups water

1 thin onion wedge (1/8 small onion)

1/4 teaspoon salt

1/4 teaspoon black peppercorns

1/4 cup gingerroot, chopped

5 garlic cloves

2 tablespoons oil

1 large onion, chopped

1 large tomato, seeded, chopped

1 teaspoon ground coriander

1 teaspoon ground cumin

1 teaspoon ground turmeric

1/4 teaspoon red (cayenne) pepper

2 bay leaves

2 cardamom pods, crushed

1-1/2 teaspoons salt

2 tablespoons plain yogurt

2 tablespoons whipping cream

1/2 teaspoon garam masala

**1/4 cup lightly packed cilantro
   leaves, chopped**

Steamed rice

Place chicken back, wing tips and neck in a pot, add water, onion wedge, 1/4 teaspoon salt and peppercorns. Bring to a boil. Reduce heat, cover and simmer 45 minutes. Strain broth and skim off fat; add water to make 2-1/2 cups broth. Set aside. In a food processor fitted with the metal blade, purée gingerroot and garlic. Heat oil in a Dutch oven. Add chopped onion; cook, stirring until lightly browned. Add gingerroot mixture; cook 3 minutes, stirring often. Add tomato; cook 3 minutes. Mix in coriander, cumin, turmeric and red pepper. Add remaining chicken pieces; cook until meat becomes firm, about 8 minutes. Add 2-1/2 cups reserved broth. Add bay leaves, cardamom pods and salt. Bring to a boil. Reduce heat, cover and simmer 30 minutes. *If making Eggplant Curry, page 108, ladle out 1 cup sauce.* For chicken curry, spoon yogurt and cream into a small cup. Gradually stir some curry sauce into yogurt mixture, then add to chicken. Stir in garam masala and bring to a boil. Stir in cilantro. Remove bay leaves. Serve over rice. Makes 4 servings.

Eggplant Curry
Kari Terung (Singapore)

The secret of the flavor is mango chutney.

1 small eggplant (about 1 lb.)
1-1/2 cups oil
1 cup sauce from Raffles'
  Anglo-Indian Chicken Curry,
  page 107
3 tablespoons mango chutney,
  chopped
Salt, if desired

Cut off stem and remove a thin slice from bottom end of eggplant. Cut eggplant crosswise into 1/2-inch-thick slices. Cut slices into strips 1/2 inch thick. Heat oil in a wok to 375F (190C). Add 1/3 of the eggplant at a time; fry until soft and lightly browned, about 8 minutes. Drain on paper towels. Eggplant may be prepared in advance to this point. When ready to serve, place eggplant in a 1-quart saucepan. Stir in curry sauce and mango chutney. Bring to a boil. Add salt to taste. Makes 4 servings.

Variation
Instead of deep-frying eggplant, place in a microwave-safe dish. Toss with 1/4 cup oil. Cover with plastic wrap; microwave on high (100%) 8 to 10 minutes or until softened.

Tapioca Pudding with Two Sauces
Gula Melaka (Singapore)

Gula Melaka *means palm sugar, which is traditionally used for one of the sauces. Dark-brown sugar is an excellent substitute.*

1/3 cup quick-cooking tapioca
2 cups water
1 (14-oz.) can coconut milk
    (1-3/4 cups)
1 cup packed dark-brown sugar
1/2 cup water
1 (1/8-inch-thick) gingerroot slice

Combine tapioca, 2 cups water and 1/4 cup coconut milk in a 1-quart saucepan; let stand 5 minutes. Chill remaining 1-1/2 cups coconut milk. Bring tapioca mixture to a boil over medium heat, stirring frequently; boil 1-1/2 minutes or until thickened. Divide among 6 (4-oz.) custard cups. Cool, then cover and refrigerate until chilled. Combine brown sugar, water and gingerroot in a small saucepan. Bring to a boil, stirring until sugar is dissolved; continue to boil 1 minute. Remove gingerroot. Cool syrup to room temperature. Unmold tapioca into small dessert bowls. Place sugar syrup and chilled coconut milk in separate pitchers. Pass with pudding to add as desired. Makes 6 servings.

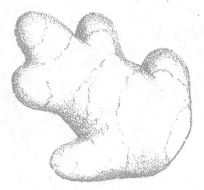

Afternoon Tea

European-style baked goods from Singapore and The Philippines are perfect teatime accompaniments. In addition to conventional hot tea, you can offer spicy ginger tea, a bracing drink that also functions as a cold remedy.

MENU
Brewed tea

Hot Ginger Tea

Finger sandwiches

Mocha Meringue Torte

Coconut Tarts

Pandan Chiffon Cake

Fruit wedges

Hot Ginger Tea

Salabat (The Philippines)

A surprising flavor that complements the rich desserts.

2 oz. gingerroot
6 cups water
1/2 cup packed light-brown sugar

Wash gingerroot thoroughly; do not peel. Thinly slice gingerroot; there should be a scant 1/2 cup. Combine gingerroot and water in a 2-quart saucepan. Bring to a boil. Boil gently, uncovered, 30 to 35 minutes or until reduced to 4 cups. Strain to remove gingerroot. Stir in sugar until dissolved. Serve hot. Makes 1 quart or 4 to 6 servings.

▲ *This sweet-and-spicy tea might be served at* merienda, *the Philippine equivalent of afternoon tea. It is also popular in Malaysia and Indonesia.*

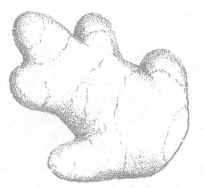

Mocha Meringue Torte

Le Gâteau Sans Rival (The Philippines)

You can also bake square- or rectangular-shaped meringue layers, making it easier to cut the torte into small squares for tea. In the Philippines, the torte is often frosted with plain buttercream. My dressier variation adds mocha flavoring and chocolate topping.

4 egg whites

1/2 cup sugar

3/4 cup unsalted cashews, toasted, finely chopped

1-1/2 teaspoons chocolate shot

Mocha Buttercream Frosting:

4 egg yolks

3/4 cup sugar

6 tablespoons water

3/4 cup butter, softened

1 oz. semisweet chocolate, melted, slightly cooled

1-1/2 teaspoons instant coffee powder

Preheat oven to 300F (150C). Place a 9-inch-round cake pan bottom down on waxed paper; trace 3 circles. Cut around tracings to make 3 circles. Invert 3 9-inch-round cake pans. Grease bottom (now the top) of each. Place waxed-paper circle on bottom. Set aside. Beat egg whites in a large bowl until soft peaks form. Beat in sugar 1 tablespoon at a time, beating until stiff and glossy. Gently fold in 1/2 cup cashews. Spoon 1/3 of meringue onto each prepared cake pan; spread evenly with a spatula. Place in oven at 5-minute intervals. Bake 50 to 60 minutes, until browned and thoroughly dry. As each layer is done, remove from oven; invert onto a large dinner plate. Carefully peel off waxed paper. Place on a rack to cool. Make Mocha Buttercream Frosting. To assemble, place 1 meringue layer flat-side up on a platter. With a spatula, spread slightly less than 1/3 of the frosting over meringue. Add a second meringue layer, flat-side down. Press remaining meringue layer, flat-side down, over frosting. Spread remaining frosting over top and sides.

Sprinkle remaining 1/4 cup chopped cashews over top, then sprinkle with chocolate shot. Cover torte loosely with waxed paper; chill until frosting is firm, about 1 hour. Cut in wedges to serve. Store any leftover torte in refrigerator. Makes 6 to 8 servings.

Mocha Buttercream Frosting:
Place egg yolks in a small bowl. Beat with an electric mixer at high speed until pale and thick. Combine sugar and water in a small saucepan. Boil until syrup forms a soft ball when a small amount is dropped into a cup of cold water (234-240F, 112-115C on a candy thermometer). With mixer at high speed, pour syrup in a very thin stream into egg yolks. After syrup is incorporated, continue to beat until outside of bowl feels cool. Set mixer at medium or creaming speed. Add butter 1 tablespoon at a time, beating until each is incorporated. When all butter is added, beat in chocolate and coffee powder. (If ingredients are slightly warm and make frosting too liquid to spread, refrigerate to firm slightly, then beat thoroughly.)

Coconut Tarts

(Singapore)

It's easy to make tarts when you don't have to roll out the dough. In this recipe, the pastry is pressed into the tart tins.

1/4 cup butter, softened
1 tablespoon sugar
1 egg yolk
1 cup all-purpose flour
2 tablespoons ice water

Coconut Filling:
2 eggs
1/2 cup sugar
1-1/2 cups flaked coconut
1/4 cup butter, melted
1/2 teaspoon vanilla extract

Preheat oven to 350F (175C). Cream butter and sugar in a medium bowl. Beat in egg yolk. Stir in flour. Mixture will be dry. Add enough ice water to make a dough that is soft but not sticky. Knead lightly; form into a ball. Divide dough into quarters. Divide each quarter into thirds, making 12 pieces of dough. Place each in center of a 2-1/2-inch fluted tart pan. With your thumbs, press dough evenly over bottom and up sides to top. Place pans on a baking sheet. Make Coconut Filling. Divide filling among tart shells. Bake 10 minutes. Reduce heat to 325F (165C); bake 15 more minutes or until golden brown. Carefully remove tarts to a rack to cool. When cooled, remove from pans, prying gently at edges with a sharp knife to loosen if necessary. Makes 12 tarts.

Coconut Filling:
Beat eggs in a medium bowl. Add sugar; beat until mixture is pale yellow. Mix in coconut, then butter. Stir in vanilla.

Pandan Chiffon Cake

(Malaysia)

This spectacular cake is tinted a spring-like green.

2 cups cake flour
1-1/2 cups sugar
1 tablespoon baking powder
1/8 teaspoon salt
7 eggs, separated
3/4 cup coconut milk
1/2 cup oil
1 teaspoon pandan or
  coconut flavoring
1/4 teaspoon green food color
1/4 teaspoon yellow food color
1 egg white
1/2 teaspoon cream of tartar
4 drops green food color
4 drops yellow food color

Whipped-Cream Frosting:
1 (8-oz.) carton whipping
  cream (1 cup)
1/4 teaspoon pandan or
  coconut flavoring
1/4 teaspoon green food color
1/4 teaspoon yellow food color
3 tablespoons sugar

Preheat oven to 325F (165C). Combine cake flour, sugar, baking powder and salt in a sifter; sift 3 times. Sift last time into a large mixer bowl. Make hollow in center; add egg yolks, coconut milk, oil, pandan flavoring and 1/4 teaspoons of food colors. Beat at low speed until dry ingredients are moistened, then at high speed until thoroughly blended. Combine 8 egg whites, cream of tartar and drops of food colors in a large bowl. Beat until stiff but not dry. Gently fold 1/4 of the egg whites into batter. Fold in remaining egg whites. Turn into an ungreased 10-inch tube pan. Bake 55 to 60 minutes or until cake tester comes out clean and top of cake springs back when lightly touched. Invert pan; let cake stand until cooled. To loosen, run a knife around outer edge of cake. Invert and turn out cake. Make Whipped-Cream Frosting. Frost top and sides of cake. Makes 10 to 12 servings.

Whipped-Cream Frosting:
Combine whipping cream, pandan flavoring and food colors in a bowl. Beat until thick. Gradually beat in sugar until very stiff.

Vietnamese-French Dinner Party

Although the French left Vietnam in 1954, the language is still widely used in Ho Chi Minh City (Saigon). Restaurants there serve onion soup gratinée, poulet roti (roast chicken) and other French classics along with Vietnamese and Chinese food.

MENU

Shrimp Soup with Pineapple

Beef Stew with Onion Rings & Mint

Buttered green beans

Parsley-sprinkled carrots

Salad with vinaigrette dressing

Hot French bread

Vietnamese Caramel Custard, page 140.

A merlot or soft cabernet sauvignon wine

Shrimp Soup with Pineapple

Canh Chua Ca (Vietnam)

This colorful southern Vietnamese soup is simultaneously sour, sweet and spicy. Green onions and fried garlic sprinkled over the top add still more flavor.

4 large garlic cloves

1/4 cup oil

2 tablespoons chopped
  green-onion tops

3 cups beef broth

1 cup water

1/4 cup white vinegar

1 (8-oz.) can pineapple chunks

1-1/2 tablespoons sugar

1 tablespoon fish sauce

1 teaspoon salt

1/8 teaspoon red (cayenne) pepper

1/4 teaspoon white pepper

1 (4-oz.) can button mushrooms,
  drained

1 small tomato, cut in eighths

24 small to medium shrimp (about
  6 oz.) shelled, deveined

1/4 lb. bean sprouts

Chop garlic; you should have about 3 tablespoons. Heat oil in a small skillet. Add garlic; fry slowly until golden, stirring frequently. Drain on paper towels. Discard oil. Set garlic and green-onion tops aside for garnish. Combine beef broth, water and vinegar in a 3-quart saucepan. Drain juice from pineapple; add to saucepan. Set drained pineapple chunks aside. Add sugar, fish sauce, salt, red pepper and white pepper to saucepan. Bring to a boil. Add pineapple chunks, mushrooms and tomato wedges; bring to a boil again. Add shrimp, reduce heat and simmer 2 minutes until shrimp turn pink. Divide bean sprouts among 4 large soup bowls. Ladle soup into bowls. Garnish each serving with reserved fried garlic and green-onion tops. Makes 4 servings.

Beef Stew with Onion Rings & Mint

Bo Kho (Vietnam)

Tasting this stew, it is hard to detect the Asian seasonings.

2 lbs. trimmed boneless beef chuck

2 tablespoons soy sauce

2 tablespoons tomato paste

2 tablespoons finely ground lemon grass (1 small stalk)

1 tablespoon soybean condiment

1 teaspoon curry powder

1 teaspoon paprika

1 teaspoon black pepper

3 bay leaves

2 tablespoons oil

2 large garlic cloves, crushed

3 cups water

1 lb. carrots, diagonally cut into 1/2-inch slices

1 large onion, cut in wedges

4 teaspoons salt

1/2 teaspoon coarsely ground black pepper

1 medium onion, sliced into rings

4 large mint sprigs

1 small lemon, cut into 4 wedges

Cut beef into 1-1/2-inch chunks. Place in a medium bowl. Stir in soy sauce, tomato paste, lemon grass, soybean condiment, curry powder, paprika, 1 teaspoon pepper and bay leaves. Cover and refrigerate at least 3 hours to blend flavors. Heat oil in a Dutch oven. Add garlic and meat; cook, stirring occasionally, 6 minutes or until meat is lightly browned. Add water; bring to a boil. Cover and simmer 1-1/2 hours, stirring several times. Add carrots and onion wedges. Cover and simmer 1 hour longer; discard bay leaves. At serving time, mix salt and coarse pepper. Divide among 4 small containers for dipping. Ladle stew into heated serving bowls. Top each serving with a few onion rings and a mint sprig. Serve with a lemon wedge. To eat, squeeze enough lemon juice over salt and pepper mixture to moisten. Dip meat and carrots as desired in seasoning mixture. Makes 4 servings.

Thai Restaurant Favorites

These dishes are well-loved standards on the menus of Thai restaurants in the United States. Preparing all of them for a single dinner would be a tour de force even for the expert cook. So extract one or two favorites, team them with rice and you will have a fine meal.

MENU

Hot & Sour Shrimp Soup

Sweet Sticky Noodles

*Thai Chicken Curry with choice of
Green or Red Curry Paste*

Garlic-Pepper Beef

Steamed rice

Fried Bananas

Thai Iced Tea

Hot & Sour Shrimp Soup

Tom Yum Goong (Thailand)

This easy version of the classic Thai soup comes from the Bussaracum restaurant in Bangkok. It takes only a few minutes to prepare.

20 medium shrimp with heads, about 1/2 lb.

1 quart water (4 cups)

10 thin gingerroot slices

2 lemon-grass stalks, sliced

3 tablespoons lemon juice

3 tablespoons fish sauce

2 to 4 small fresh green chiles, sliced

4 kaffir lime leaves, coarsely broken

1/2 teaspoon salt

2 tablespoons cilantro leaves

Shell shrimp, leaving on heads. Remove sand veins. Bring water to a boil in a 2-quart saucepan. Add gingerroot and lemon grass. Holding each shrimp over saucepan, remove head, allowing juices from head portion to drop into water. Discard head. Add remainder of shrimp to saucepan. Bring to a boil. Add lemon juice, fish sauce, chiles, lime leaves and salt. Boil 2 minutes or just until shrimp turn pink. Ladle into individual bowls. Top each serving with cilantro leaves. Makes 4 servings.

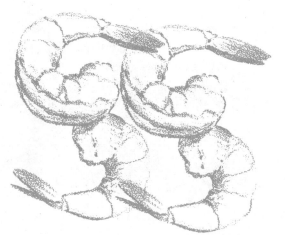

Sweet Sticky Noodles
Mee Krob (Thailand)

Crisp and sweet, these are hard to resist. The crucial step is boiling the sauce to a thick glaze. If the sauce has too much liquid, the noodles will be soggy.

1/2 cup sugar
1/4 cup water
1-1/2 tablespoons ketchup
1 tablespoon tomato paste
1 tablespoon lemon juice
1 tablespoon fish sauce
2 tablespoons shredded carrot
1/2 egg, beaten (2 tablespoons)
1/4 teaspoon all-purpose flour
1-1/2 cups oil
4 oz. thin rice-stick noodles
6 shallots or 1/2 onion, chopped
3 large garlic cloves, minced
16 shrimp, shelled, deveined
1 teaspoon fish sauce
Dash black pepper
1/4 lb. bean sprouts
1/2 cup lightly packed cilantro sprigs

Combine sugar, water, ketchup, tomato paste, lemon juice and 1 tablespoon fish sauce in a cup; set aside. Boil carrot in water 1 minute. Drain and set aside. Combine egg and flour in a small bowl; set aside. Heat oil in a wok. Break up a handful of rice sticks and drop into oil. Press with a spatula to submerge. Instantly, rice sticks will puff. Drain on paper towels. Remove noodle bits from oil. Whisk egg mixture, then pour into oil. Fry until lightly browned. Remove and drain on paper towels; set aside. Drain and reserve oil from wok; clean wok. Reheat 1-1/2 tablespoons oil in wok. Add shallots or onion and garlic; cook until lightly browned. Add shrimp; cook 2 to 3 minutes. Stir in 1 teaspoon fish sauce and pepper. Place mixture on a plate. Add sugar mixture to wok; boil until reduced to a glaze, about 5 minutes. Mixture must be almost dry. Add shrimp to glaze. Turn off heat. Add rice sticks and stir, breaking up noodles slightly. Place on a platter; press into a mound. Garnish with bean sprouts, carrots and cilantro sprigs. Place egg on top of noodles. Top with bean sprouts. Makes 6 to 8 servings.

Thai Chicken Curry

Gaeng Ped Gai (Thailand)

This recipe gives you two dishes in one. Simply switch from Green to Red Curry Paste for a change in flavor.

4 chicken-breast halves, boned, skinned, or 6 chicken thighs, skinned, trimmed of fat

2 (14-oz.) cans coconut milk

1/3 cup Green Curry Paste, page 15, or 3 to 4 tablespoons Red Curry Paste, page 16

2 Oriental eggplant, sliced into 12 slices each, or 3/4 cup tiny Thai eggplant (makhua puong)

2 tablespoons fish sauce

1 teaspoon salt

1 teaspoon sugar

1 cup lightly packed basil leaves

6 kaffir lime leaves, finely shredded

1 or 2 small fresh red or green chiles, slivered, if desired

Steamed rice

Cut chicken breasts into 1/2-inch-wide strips or bite-size pieces. Thighs may be cut up or left whole. Spoon 1/2 cup of the thickest coconut milk from top of a can that has not been shaken, into a Dutch oven. Heat over medium heat. Add curry paste; fry, stirring constantly, 2 minutes. Stir in remaining coconut milk; bring to a boil. Add chicken, eggplant, fish sauce, salt and sugar. Bring to a boil. Reduce heat, cover and simmer 30 minutes for chicken breasts, 45 minutes for thighs. Add basil and lime leaves; cook, uncovered, 1 minute. Stir in chiles, if desired. Spoon into a heated serving bowl. Serve with steamed rice. Makes 4 to 6 servings.

Garlic-Pepper Beef

Nua Katim (Thailand)

*Thai restaurants also make this dish
with pork, chicken or shrimp.*

1 lb. beef flank steak,
   partially frozen
4 garlic cloves
1/2 cup lightly packed
   cilantro leaves
1 tablespoon soy sauce
1-1/2 tablespoons water
1-1/4 teaspoons coarsely ground
   black pepper
1/2 teaspoon sugar
1/3 cup water
4 teaspoons fish sauce
1/2 teaspoon cornstarch
1 tablespoon water
3 tablespoons oil
1 small onion, halved lengthwise,
   cut into 8 wedges

Diagonally cut steak into thin slices. Place in a medium bowl. In a mortar, pound garlic and 1/4 cup of the cilantro leaves to a paste. Stir in soy sauce, 1-1/2 tablespoons water, pepper and sugar; spoon onto steak. Let stand 30 minutes. Combine 1/3 cup water and fish sauce in a small bowl; set aside. Blend cornstarch and remaining 1 tablespoon water in a separate bowl; set aside. Heat a wok. Add oil and heat. Add steak; cook, stirring, until no longer pink. Boil until liquid evaporates. Add fish-sauce mixture and onion; cook, stirring, 1 minute. Stir cornstarch mixture to blend. Add to wok; cook, stirring, until sauce thickens slightly. Spoon onto a heated platter; arrange remaining 1/4 cup cilantro leaves in center. Makes 4 servings.

Fried Bananas
Klouy Tod (Thailand)

Fried bananas are popular throughout Thailand. Usually, the bananas are sliced lengthwise, but this version from a resort in the province of Chiang Mai calls for banana chunks and adds an extra touch—a lime-flavored syrup.

1/4 cup all-purpose flour
1 teaspoon baking powder
1/4 teaspoon salt
1/2 cup water
1 teaspoon oil
4 large medium-ripe bananas
1-1/2 cups oil

Syrup:
1/2 cup sugar
1 cup boiling water
1 (2 x 3/4-inch) lime- or lemon-peel strip, green or yellow part only

Make Syrup; set aside. Sift flour, baking powder and salt into a medium bowl. Beat in water and 1 teaspoon oil until smooth. Peel bananas. Cut each crosswise into 4 chunks. Heat oil in a wok or medium skillet to 360F (180C) or until a 1-inch bread cube turns golden brown in 60 seconds. Dip each banana chunk in batter, then place in oil. Spoon a little batter over top. Fry until golden on each side, 3 to 4 minutes, turning as needed. Drain on paper towels. Serve at once, passing syrup to spoon over as desired. Makes 4 servings.

Syrup:
Heat sugar in a small saucepan until sugar is melted, clear and golden in color. Slowly stir in boiling water; sugar will bubble up and thicken but will dissolve again. Stir until smooth. Bring to a boil, add lime or lemon peel and boil 10 minutes until syrup is reduced to 3/4 cup. Let cool to room temperature.

Thai Iced Tea

Cha Yen (Thailand)

Surprise your guests with an unusual sweet drink.

3-1/2 cups water
1/3 cup imported Thai tea leaves
1/3 cup sugar
1/3 cup sweetened condensed milk
1/2 cup half and half
About 4 cups crushed ice

Place water in a large saucepan; bring to a boil. Place tea leaves in a cloth coffee bag. Pour water through tea into another large container. Pour back through leaves into pan. Repeat pouring 4 more times. Stir sugar, condensed milk and half and half into tea. Pour into a 1-quart jar. Cover and refrigerate until chilled. For each serving, place 1 cup or more crushed ice in a tall glass. Pour 1 cup tea mixture over ice. Serve with straws. Makes 1 quart or 4 servings.

▲ *Proper brewing of the tea requires pouring it several times through a cloth coffee bag. The bags can be found in Latin markets as well as Thai grocery stores.*

Thai
Patio Dinner

Make your outdoor entertaining really different with a light and colorful Thai menu. Rice presented in pineapple shells is one of the attractions.

MENU

Siamese Kiss Cocktail

Barbecued Chicken

Shrimp & Young-Corn Salad

Lada's Cucumber Salad

Pineapple Rice

Mangoes & Sticky Rice
or
Frozen Lychees

Siamese Kiss

(Thailand)

This drink originated at Bussaracum, a leading restaurant in Bangkok.

1/2 oz. (1 tablespoon) light rum
1/2 oz. (1 tablespoon) tequila
1/2 oz. (1 tablespoon) cherry brandy
1/2 oz. (1 tablespoon) Grand Marnier
1-1/2 oz. (3 tablespoons) orange juice
2 teaspoons lemon juice
1/2 teaspoon Simple Syrup, page 18
Ice cubes
Lime slice and maraschino cherry
  for garnish

In a large cocktail glass, stir all ingredients except ice cubes and garnishes. Add ice cubes. Insert a wooden pick through lime slice and cherry; use to garnish drink. Makes 1 serving.

▲ *Located on a quiet lane near busy Silom Road, the restaurant Bussaracum is a pretty, peaceful place in which to take refuge from Bangkok's noisy traffic. During one such escape I began lunch with this drink.*

Barbecued Chicken
Gai Yang (Thailand)

A sweet and spicy dip makes the chicken addictive.

1 (3-lb.) chicken
3 to 4 garlic cloves
1 teaspoon salt
1/4 cup soy sauce
1 tablespoon water

Sweet & Sour Red-Chile Sauce:
3/4 cup sugar
3/4 cup distilled white vinegar
1 small fresh red chile, stemmed, seeded, finely chopped
1/2 teaspoon salt

Cut up chicken. Separate thighs from drumsticks. Cut breast in half crosswise. Place in a shallow pan or glass dish. Pound garlic with salt in a mortar until reduced to a paste. Blend in soy sauce. Turn mixture into a small cup. Rinse out mortar with the water; add to mixture. Rub evenly over chicken pieces. Cover and marinate in refrigerator 2 hours. Bring to room temperature before grilling. Prepare barbecue. Place chicken skin-side down on grill over hot coals; cook, turning to brown evenly, 30 to 40 minutes, depending upon size of pieces, or until juices run clear when meat is pierced. Serve with individual bowls of Sweet & Sour Red Chile Sauce for dipping or to spoon over chicken. Makes 4 servings.

Sweet & Sour Red-Chile Sauce: Combine all ingredients in small saucepan. Boil until reduced to 2/3 cup. Serve warm or at room temperature.

Shrimp & Corn Salad

Yam Kao Pode On (Thailand)

*This Bangkok salad is low in calories;
the dressing consists solely of vinegar.
You can double the recipe for a party.*

**1/2 lb. small to medium shrimp,
shelled, deveined**

**1 (15-oz.) can young corn, drained,
rinsed**

1/2 cup sliced celery

1/4 cup sliced green onions

**2 small fresh green chiles,
thinly sliced**

3 garlic cloves, minced

1/4 cup white vinegar

1/4 teaspoon salt

Dash white pepper

**2 leaves romaine, salad-bowl or
other leafy lettuce**

1 medium tomato

Bring 2 cups salted water to a boil
in a 1-quart saucepan. Add shrimp;
cook 3 minutes or until pink. Drain;
rinse with water. Cut corn
diagonally into 1/2-inch-thick slices.
Combine shrimp, corn, celery, green
onions, chiles and garlic in a
medium bowl. Add vinegar, salt and
pepper. Mix lightly but thoroughly.
Cover and marinate in refrigerator 2
hours or longer. To serve, place
lettuce leaves end to end on platter.
Spoon salad into center. Thinly slice
tomato and arrange on each side.
Makes 4 small servings.

Lada's Cucumber Salad

Ajar (Thailand)

This spicy relish is served with satay, barbecued chicken or other Thai dishes.

3 tablespoons rice vinegar

1 tablespoon sugar

1/2 teaspoon salt

Dash black pepper

1 (8-oz.) cucumber, peeled

1/2 cup thinly sliced red onion (cut slices into thirds or quarters before measuring)

2 tablespoons cilantro leaves, chopped

1 small fresh red or green chile, sliced

In a medium bowl, stir vinegar, sugar, salt and pepper until sugar and salt are dissolved. Quarter cucumber lengthwise. Remove seeds. Cut quarters crosswise into 1/8-inch-thick slices. Add cucumber, onion, cilantro and chile to vinegar dressing; toss until combined. Cover and marinate in refrigerator 3 hours, stirring occasionally. Makes 4 servings.

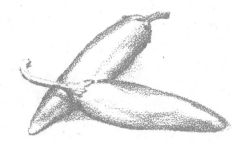

Pineapple Rice
Kao Pad Supparod (Thailand)

Buy a large pineapple, cut it in half lengthwise and scoop out the fruit. Use the shells as containers for the rice.

1 Chinese sausage
1/2 cup water
12 medium shrimp,
  shelled, deveined
1 tablespoon oil
1/4 medium onion, finely chopped
1 garlic clove, minced
1-1/2 teaspoons salt
1 cup long-grain rice, cooked,
  refrigerated overnight
2 tablespoons golden raisins,
  softened in hot water, drained
1 egg
1/2 cup diced fresh pineapple
2 green onions, chopped

Place sausage and 1/2 cup water in a small skillet; bring to a boil. Reduce heat, cover and simmer 10 minutes, turning sausage after 5 minutes. Drain sausage; cut diagonally into thin slices. and set aside. Cook shrimp in boiling salted water 3 minutes or until pink. Drain; set aside. Heat a wok over medium-high heat. Add oil and heat. Add onion; cook until tender but not browned. Add garlic; cook a few seconds to flavor oil. Add salt, then rice; toss until rice is heated. Push rice to 1 side of wok. Add sausage, shrimp and drained raisins. Stir until heated, then toss to mix with rice. Make a well in center. Break egg into well, stir until scrambled, then mix with rice. Make well again, pushing rice mixture up side of wok. Add pineapple. Cook until heated, then mix with rice. Stir in green onions. Spoon into a serving dish or pineapple shells. Makes 4 to 6 servings.

Mangoes & Sticky Rice

Kaoneo Mamoung (Thailand)

A wonderful dessert that makes mango season worth waiting for. The Thais sprinkle the rice with crunchy roasted mung beans. Toasted sesame seeds are just as good.

1 cup white glutinous rice
1 (14-oz.) can coconut milk
  (1-3/4 cups)
1/3 cup sugar
3/4 teaspoon salt
2 medium to large mangoes
1 teaspoon toasted sesame seeds

Frozen Lychees
Lynchee Loy Kao (Thailand)
1 (20-oz.) can lychees in
  heavy syrup
Place can in freezer; freeze until solid, several hours or overnight. Open can and let lychees soften slightly before serving. Spoon into 4 dessert bowls. Makes 4 servings.

Wash rice; place in a bowl. Cover with cold water; soak 4 to 6 hours. Drain well. Place in a colander or sieve with fine holes. Set colander on a rack over water in a large pot; water must not touch rice. Cover pot; bring water to a boil. Reduce heat slightly; steam rice 25 minutes. Meanwhile, open can of coconut milk carefully without shaking. Spoon off 1/4 cup of thick milk that has risen to the top. Place in a small bowl, cover and refrigerate. Stir remaining coconut milk to blend. Measure 1/2 cup; reserve remainder for another use. Stir coconut milk, sugar and salt in a bowl until sugar is dissolved. Remove rice from steamer. Spoon into a 1-1/2-quart baking dish. Stir sugar mixture into rice. Cover, return to steamer and steam 10 more minutes. Remove baking dish to a rack. Let rice cool, covered, to room temperature. Peel mangoes; slice pulp. Divide rice among dessert plates. Top with 1 tablespoon reserved thick coconut milk. Sprinkle with sesame seeds. Garnish with mango slices. Makes 4 servings.

Philippine Fiesta

Filipinos celebrate any occasion with a party, and a party means lots of food, set out in a lavish buffet. Often guests bring along their specialties, and lively talk about recipes becomes part of the entertainment. In the Islands, spring is fiesta season and the occasion for many gatherings.

MENU

Fried Egg Rolls

Tangy Pork Soup

Mike's Special Chicken Adobo

Stir-Fried Rice Noodles with Pork

Garlic Rice

Green-Papaya Relish

Strawberry Flan

Fried Egg Rolls
Lumpia (The Philippines)

The vinegar-garlic dip distinguishes lumpia from Chinese egg rolls.

1 tablespoon oil
1 small onion, finely chopped
3 large garlic cloves, crushed, then minced
1 lb. boneless lean pork, ground
1/4 lb. green cabbage, shredded (1-1/2 cups packed)
1/4 lb. bean sprouts
1 teaspoon salt
16 lumpia or egg-roll wrappers
3 cups oil

Vinegar Dip:
1/2 cup white vinegar
1/4 cup water
2 large garlic cloves, minced
1/2 teaspoon salt

Heat 1 tablespoon oil in a large skillet. Add onion and garlic; sauté. Add pork; cook and stir until no longer pink. Add cabbage and bean sprouts; cook until wilted. Stir in salt. Cool before filling wrappers. Prepare Vinegar Dip. Place egg-roll wrapper with a point at bottom. Place 1/4 cup filling on wrapper above point, spreading filling slightly. Filling should be in line with or below side points. Brush edges from side points to top with water. Fold bottom point over filling. Fold side points to center. Roll up to top. Continue filling wrappers. If preparing in advance, stack, cover tightly and refrigerate. Bring to room temperature before frying. Heat 3 cups oil in a wok to 360F (180C). Fry 4 at a time 4 to 6 minutes until golden brown on both sides. Drain excess oil from lumpia over wok, then drain on paper towels. Cut in thirds to serve. Serve with Vinegar Dip. Makes 16 lumpia or 48 pieces.

Vinegar Dip:
Combine ingredients. Let stand to blend flavors.

Tangy Pork Soup

Sinigang na Baboy (The Philippines)

Served with steamed rice, this soup makes a hearty supper. Spinach may be substituted for the kangkong.

1-1/2 lbs. pork shoulder-blade meat or other boneless pork

8 cups water

2 medium tomatoes, cut into wedges

1 medium onion, cut into wedges

1 or 2 small green chiles

4 teaspoons salt

1/2 lb. white radish (daikon) or turnip, peeled

1/4 lb. Chinese yard-long or green beans

1/4 lb. kangkong, tops only, or spinach

1/4 cup lemon juice

Steamed rice

Fish sauce

Trim fat from pork; cut pork into 1-1/2-inch chunks. Place in a 4-quart saucepan. Add water; bring to a boil. Skim off foam from surface until clear. Reduce heat. Add tomatoes, onion, chiles and salt. Cover and simmer 45 minutes. Cut radish in half lengthwise, then cut crosswise into 1/2-inch slices. Remove ends of beans. Cut beans into 1-1/2-inch lengths; add to soup with radish. Cover; cook 20 minutes. Add kangkong or spinach. Cook 5 minutes. Stir in lemon juice. Serve soup in large bowls. Accompany with plates of steamed rice. To eat, spoon portions of the soup ingredients and broth over the rice. Season to taste with fish sauce. Eat remaining broth from the bowls. Makes 6 to 8 servings.

Mike's Special Chicken Adobo
(The Philippines)

There are many versions of the Philippine dish, adobo. Often pork is used; sometimes chicken and pork are combined. Some recipes add coconut milk. Lemon juice replaces the usual tangy seasoning, vinegar. The finishing touch is a bed of spinach cooked in the pan juices.

1 bunch spinach
8 chicken thighs
3 tablespoons soy sauce
2 large garlic cloves, minced
1/4 teaspoon freshly ground pepper
1 small bay leaf
1/4 cup lemon juice
Lemon wedges

Wash spinach well; drain. Discard coarse stems. Place chicken thighs in a single layer, skin side down, in a large deep skillet. Cook, covered, over medium heat 10 minutes. Add soy sauce, garlic, pepper and bay leaf. Cover and simmer 35 minutes. Turn chicken at least twice. Cover and cook 5 minutes. Remove chicken. Add spinach leaves and cook in pan juices until just wilted. Place spinach on a heated platter. Arrange chicken on top of spinach. Garnish with lemon wedges. Makes 4 servings.

Stir-Fried Rice Noodles with Pork

Pancit Bihon (The Philippines)

A cook in a small town outside Manila prepared these noodles for a late-afternoon snack.

6 oz. rice-stick noodles

2 tablespoons oil

2 garlic cloves, minced

1/4 lb. lean pork, cut into thin strips

4 tablespoons soy sauce

1/2 cup chicken broth

1/4 lb. green cabbage (1/4 small head), cored, finely sliced

1/4 cup finely shredded carrot

1/4 cup finely chopped onion

1/4 teaspoon freshly ground black pepper

2 green onions, chopped

1 small lime, cut into 4 wedges

Soak rice sticks in a medium bowl in water to cover 30 minutes. Drain well. Heat a wok over high heat. Add oil and heat. Add garlic, then pork; stir-fry 2 minutes. Add 1 tablespoon soy sauce; stir-fry 2 minutes longer or until pork has absorbed soy sauce. Add broth and additional 1 tablespoon soy sauce. Stir in cabbage, carrot and onion. Cover; cook 2 minutes. Add noodles, remaining 2 tablespoons soy sauce and pepper. Cook, stirring, 2 minutes or until noodles have absorbed liquid in wok. Spoon onto a heated platter. Sprinkle green onions over top. Serve with lime wedges to squeeze onto noodles as desired. Makes 4 servings.

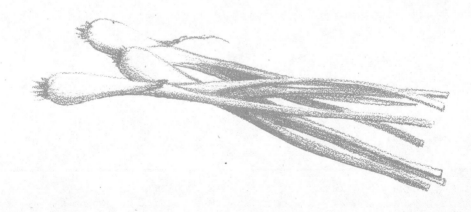

Garlic Rice

Sinangag (The Philippines)

A simple side dish, ready in minutes.

1 tablespoon oil
2 medium garlic cloves, minced
1/2 teaspoon salt, or to taste
1 cup long-grain rice, cooked, cooled

Heat a wok over medium heat. Add oil and heat. Add garlic and salt; fry until fragrant and oil is flavored, being careful not to burn garlic. Add rice and cook until heated through, stirring gently. Makes 4 servings.

▲ *This rice, served with dried fish, sausage or other meats, is a breakfast staple in the Philippines. Some cooks fry the garlic just long enough to flavor the oil. Others like it golden brown and crisp.*

Green-Papaya Relish

Papayang Atsara (The Philippines)

*Green papayas have very pale,
green-white flesh. If you can't find one,
try the sauerkraut variation.*

**1 green (unripe) papaya, about
    1-1/4 lbs.**
1 tablespoon salt
3 cups boiling water
1/2 cup white vinegar
1/4 cup sugar
3/4 teaspoon salt
Dash white pepper
1/4 red bell pepper, finely shredded
1/4 cup small onion, finely shredded
**1/2 small carrot, finely shredded
    (1/4 cup)**

Quarter papaya lengthwise; peel. Scoop out and discard seeds. Cut papaya into long fine shreds, using shredding or julienne blade of a food processor or hand grater. Place in a medium bowl. Add salt; squeeze with your hands until papaya becomes very juicy. Pour boiling water over papaya; let stand 10 minutes. Pour into a sieve, drain and rinse well. Squeeze out as much water as possible from papaya. Place in a medium bowl. Combine vinegar, sugar, salt and white pepper in a small saucepan. Bring to a boil. Add bell pepper, onion and carrot. Remove from heat; stir 30 seconds. Pour over papaya; stir until combined. Cover and refrigerate until chilled. Makes 2 cups.

Variation
Substitute 1 (1-lb.) can sauerkraut for papaya. Pour sauerkraut into a sieve; rinse and drain well, squeezing out excess water. Place in a bowl. Add vinegar dressing and shredded vegetables; mix well, cover and chill.

Strawberry Flan
(The Philippines)

A pretty springtime dessert.

1/3 cup sugar

2 cups half and half

3 eggs

1/2 cup sugar

1/2 teaspoon vanilla extract

24 to 32 strawberries (4 berries per
   serving), hulled, thinly sliced

Custard Sauce:

2 eggs

3 tablespoons sugar

1-3/4 cups milk

1/2 teaspoon vanilla extract

Vietnamese Caramel Custard
Prepare as directed above. Bake
flan in individual custard cups.
Chill; unmold and top each
serving with cracked ice. Omit
strawberries and sauce.

Preheat oven to 325F (165C). Heat
1/3 cup sugar in a small skillet until
melted, clear and golden in color.
Spoon over bottom and partway up
sides of an 8 x 4-inch loaf pan.
Combine half and half, eggs, 1/2 cup
sugar and vanilla in a blender. Blend
at high speed 20 seconds. Pour into
prepared pan. Set in a larger baking
pan. Add hot water to come halfway
up sides of loaf pan. Bake 1 hour or
until a knife inserted slightly
off-center comes out clean. Cool,
cover and refrigerate. Flan may be
made a day ahead of serving. Make
Custard Sauce. With a knife, loosen
edges of flan. Turn out onto a platter.
Cut into cubes. Garnish strawberries.
Spoon Custard Sauce over top.
Makes 6 to 8 servings.

Custard Sauce:
Beat eggs with sugar in top of a
double boiler. Scald milk in a
saucepan. Gradually beat milk into
egg mixture. Place over simmering
water; cook, stirring constantly, until
mixture thickens slightly, 20 to 25
minutes. Remove from heat; stir in
vanilla. Pour into a bowl, cover and
refrigerate until chilled. Makes about
1-3/4 cups.